20th-CENTURY IRISH POEMS

55

m

20th-CENTURY IRISH POEMS

Selected by MICHAEL LONGLEY

ff

faber and faber

First published in 2002
by Faber and Faber Limited
3 Queen Square London WC1N 3AU
Published in the United States by Faber and Faber Inc.,
an affiliate of Farrar, Straus and Giroux LLC, New York

Photoset by Wilmaset Ltd, Birkenhead, Wirral
Printed in Italy

A CIP record for this book
is available from the British Library

ISBN 0–571–20941–6

10 9 8 7 6 5 4 3 2 1

Contents

Preface

This is a selection of one hundred Irish poems published in the last century. It does not intend to be canonical. (Its scale prevents that.) Since 1987 I have written into a common-place book poems which have startled and moved me. Some are included here. This anthology results from decades of random reading plus a recent deliberate trawl to discover more examples of what Robert Graves calls 'heart-rending sense', poems I would want to copy out in longhand or learn by heart or share with others in a book like this one.

Pressure of space licenses me to indulge my own preference for the intensity of the lyric. With more pages I would have represented such keystone long poems as Patrick Kavanagh's 'The Great Hunger', Louis MacNeice's 'Autumn Journal', Paul Muldoon's 'The More a Man Has'. I would also have included more poems in Irish (presentation in two languages affording less leeway). The mutually enriching collaboration between Irish language and English language poets has boosted Irish as a cultural force and helped to save it from being exploited as a political pawn. It has also reminded English language poets of their cultural whereabouts.

Though I hope to give the reader the pleasure of finding unfamiliar work, I have put in, for different reasons, some well-known pieces. 'Father and Son' is simply F. R. Higgins's finest lyric; all of Patrick Kavanagh's dozen best poems are collector's items; Derek Mahon's 'A Disused Shed in Co. Wexford' is, for me, the greatest Irish poem since Yeats; the two poems by Austin Clarke are among my own all-time favourites; the will-o'-the-wisp beauty of Padraic Colum's 'She Moved Through the Fair' reminds us that Irish poetry's deep roots in song and story have helped to keep it lively.

The first poet represented here was born in 1852; the last, one hundred and ten years later. That seems a fair span. Poets born after the mid-1960s will have to wait for another anthology. Several of their first and second collections have impressed me. Their future work will interpret an Ireland which has been changing with bewildering speed. Out and about at the beginning of the twenty-first century we see few of the haystacks and thatched roofs which belong to earlier Irish poetic landscapes. Contaminated lakes, fish-kills, ruthless overgrazing, 'bungalow blitz', the relentless degradation of a beautiful island – all of this awaits its laureates. Not that I would dismiss as 'cloud-shadow connoisseurs' (Tim Robinson's devastating phrase) any of the poets I have gathered together here.

Throughout these pages history makes its presence felt, sometimes in close-up, sometimes as noises-off: emigration, the 1916 Uprising, World War, the Troubles, the hunger strikes. Within the swirls of political turbulence slower processes of social change condition the language and structure of poetry – urbanisation, the women's movement, the search for new forms of spiritual meaning as institutional religion implodes. This affects even the most intimate writing, the fine love poems and elegies which continue to emblazon the extraordinary Irish achievement. The diversity of verse-shape, voice-tone and word-music shows that there are many ways in which a poem can be a poem. And there are just as many ways of being Irish or, more precisely, having an imaginative relationship with Ireland.

Michael Longley
Belfast, May Day 2001

20th-CENTURY IRISH POEMS

IN MEMORIAM

Seán Dunne
Michael Hartnett
James Simmons

I don't expect to touch the sky with my two hands.

Sappho

Donal Óg

(from the Irish)

O Donal Óg, if you go across the sea,
Bring myself with you and do not forget it;
And you will have a sweetheart for fair days and market days,
And the daughter of the King of Greece beside you at night.

It is late last night the dog was speaking of you;
The snipe was speaking of you in her deep marsh.
It is you are the lonely bird through the woods;
And that you may be without a mate until you find me.

You promised me, and you said a lie to me,
That you would be before me where the sheep are flocked;
I gave a whistle and three hundred cries to you,
And I found nothing there but a bleating lamb.

You promised me a thing that was hard for you,
A ship of gold under a silver mast;
Twelve towns with a market in all of them,
And a fine white court by the side of the sea.

You promised me a thing that is not possible,
That you would give me gloves of the skin of a fish;
That you would give me shoes of the skin of a bird;
And a suit of the dearest silk in Ireland.

O Donal Óg, it is I would be better to you
Than a high, proud, spendthrift lady:
I would milk the cow; I would bring help to you;
And if you were hard pressed, I would strike a blow for you.

O, ochone, and it's not with hunger
Or with wanting food, or drink, or sleep,
That I am growing thin, and my life is shortened;
But it is the love of a young man has withered me away.

It is early in the morning that I saw him coming,
Going along the road on the back of a horse;
He did not come to me; he made nothing of me;
And it is on my way home that I cried my fill.

When I go by myself to the Well of Loneliness,
I sit down and I go through my trouble;
When I see the world and do not see my boy,
He that has an amber shade in his hair.

It was on that Sunday I gave my love to you;
The Sunday that is last before Easter Sunday.
And myself on my knees reading the Passion;
And my two eyes giving love to you for ever.

O, aya! my mother, give myself to him;
And give him all that you have in the world;
Get out yourself to ask for alms,
And do not come back and forward looking for me.

My mother said to me not to be talking with you today,
Or tomorrow, or on Sunday;
It was a bad time she took for telling me that;
It was shutting the door after the house was robbed.

My heart is as black as the blackness of the sloe,
Or as the black coal that is on the smith's forge;
Or as the sole of a shoe left in white halls;
It was you put that darkness over my life.

You have taken the east from me; you have taken the west
  from me;
You have taken what is before me and what is behind me;
You have taken the moon, you have taken the sun from me,
And my fear is great that you have taken God from me!

KATHARINE TYNAN

The Cattle

As we sped homewards under a starry sky,
   By the rich pastures, the sleeping and quiet trees,
What are the little lights, tossed low and high
   As a lantern swung in a man's hand? What are these?

Who are these coming? A soundless multitude
   Swerving away from the light? These are eyes, eyes, eyes,
The eyes of frightened cattle, red as blood,
   Pass into the night and its mysteries.

Under the holy mountains the pastures keep
   Dew and honey and quiet breathing, deep rest,
By the side of the milky mother the lambs are asleep
   Till the cuckoo calls; the night has a mother's breast.

But these that have passed us by; they go, they go,
   Driven with curses and goads, unpitied, unstayed
To the slaughter house and the blood and at last the blow –
   The ghostly cattle passing have made me afraid.

The Wild Swans at Coole

The trees are in their autumn beauty,
The woodland paths are dry,
Under the October twilight the water
Mirrors a still sky;
Upon the brimming water among the stones
Are nine-and-fifty swans.

The nineteenth autumn has come upon me
Since I first made my count:
I saw, before I had well finished,
All suddenly mount
And scatter wheeling in great broken rings
Upon their clamorous wings.

I have looked upon those brilliant creatures
And now my heart is sore.
All's changed since I, hearing at twilight,
The first time on this shore,
The bell-beat of their wings above my head,
Trod with a lighter tread.

Unwearied still, lover by lover,
They paddle in the cold
Companionable streams or climb the air;
Their hearts have not grown old;
Passion or conquest, wander where they will,
Attend upon them still.

But now they drift on the still water,
Mysterious, beautiful;
Among what rushes will they build,
By what lake's edge or pool
Delight men's eyes when I awake some day
To find they have flown away?

Broken Dreams

There is grey in your hair.
Young men no longer suddenly catch their breath
When you are passing;
But maybe some old gaffer mutters a blessing
Because it was your prayer
Recovered him upon the bed of death.
For your sole sake – that all heart's ache have known,
And given to others all heart's ache,
From meagre girlhood's putting on
Burdensome beauty – for your sole sake
Heaven has put away the stroke of her doom,
So great her portion in that peace you make
By merely walking in a room.

Your beauty can but leave among us
Vague memories, nothing but memories.
A young man when the old men are done talking
Will say to an old man, 'Tell me of that lady
The poet stubborn with his passion sang us
When age might well have chilled his blood.'

Vague memories, nothing but memories,
But in the grave all, all, shall be renewed.
The certainty that I shall see that lady
Leaning or standing or walking
In the first loveliness of womanhood,
And with the fervour of my youthful eyes,
Has set me muttering like a fool.

You are more beautiful than any one,
And yet your body had a flaw:
Your small hands were not beautiful,
And I am afraid that you will run
And paddle to the wrist

In that mysterious, always brimming lake
Where those that have obeyed the holy law
Paddle and are perfect. Leave unchanged
The hands that I have kissed,
For old sake's sake.

The last stroke of midnight dies.
All day in the one chair
From dream to dream and rhyme to rhyme I have ranged
In rambling talk with an image of air:
Vague memories, nothing but memories.

To a Squirrel at Kyle-na-no

Come play with me;
Why should you run
Through the shaking tree
As though I'd a gun
To strike you dead?
When all I would do
Is to scratch your head
And let you go.

Easter 1916

I have met them at close of day
Coming with vivid faces
From counter or desk among grey
Eighteenth-century houses.
I have passed with a nod of the head
Or polite meaningless words,
Or have lingered awhile and said
Polite meaningless words,
And thought before I had done
Of a mocking tale or a gibe

To please a companion
Around the fire at the club,
Being certain that they and I
But lived where motley is worn:
All changed, changed utterly:
A terrible beauty is born.

That woman's days were spent
In ignorant good-will,
Her nights in argument
Until her voice grew shrill.
What voice more sweet than hers
When, young and beautiful,
She rode to harriers?
This man had kept a school
And rode our wingèd horse;
This other his helper and friend
Was coming into his force;
He might have won fame in the end,
So sensitive his nature seemed,
So daring and sweet his thought.
This other man I had dreamed
A drunken, vainglorious lout.
He had done most bitter wrong
To some who are near my heart,
Yet I number him in the song;
He, too, has resigned his part
In the casual comedy;
He, too, has been changed in his turn,
Transformed utterly:
A terrible beauty is born.

Hearts with one purpose alone
Through summer and winter seem
Enchanted to a stone
To trouble the living stream.
The horse that comes from the road,

The rider, the birds that range
From cloud to tumbling cloud,
Minute by minute they change;
A shadow of cloud on the stream
Changes minute by minute;
A horse-hoof slides on the brim,
And a horse plashes within it;
The long-legged moor-hens dive,
And hens to moor-cocks call;
Minute by minute they live:
The stone's in the midst of all.

Too long a sacrifice
Can make a stone of the heart.
O when may it suffice?
That is Heaven's part, our part
To murmur name upon name,
As a mother names her child
When sleep at last has come
On limbs that had run wild.
What is it but nightfall?
No, no, not night but death;
Was it needless death after all?
For England may keep faith
For all that is done and said.
We know their dream; enough
To know they dreamed and are dead;
And what if excess of love
Bewildered them till they died?
I write it out in a verse –
MacDonagh and MacBride
And Connolly and Pearse
Now and in time to be,
Wherever green is worn,

Are changed, changed utterly:
A terrible beauty is born.

September 25, 1916

A Last Confession

What lively lad most pleasured me
Of all that with me lay?
I answer that I gave my soul
And loved in misery,
But had great pleasure with a lad
That I loved bodily.

Flinging from his arms I laughed
To think his passion such
He fancied that I gave a soul
Did but our bodies touch,
And laughed upon his breast to think
Beast gave beast as much.

I gave what other women gave
That stepped out of their clothes,
But when this soul, its body off,
Naked to naked goes,
He it has found shall find therein
What none other knows,

And give his own and take his own
And rule in his own right;
And though it loved in misery
Close and cling so tight,
There's not a bird of day that dare
Extinguish that delight.

High Talk

Processions that lack high stilts have nothing that catches
the eye.
What if my great-granddad had a pair that were twenty foot
high,
And mine were but fifteen foot, no modern stalks upon
higher,
Some rogue of the world stole them to patch up a fence or a
fire.
Because piebald ponies, led bears, caged lions, make but
poor shows,
Because children demand Daddy-long-legs upon his timber
toes,
Because women in the upper storeys demand a face at the
pane,
That patching old heels they may shriek, I take to chisel and
plane.

Malachi Stilt-Jack am I, whatever I learned has run wild,
From collar to collar, from stilt to stilt, from father to child,
All metaphor, Malachi, stilts and all. A barnacle goose
Far up in the stretches of night; night splits and the dawn
breaks loose;
I, through the terrible novelty of light, stalk on, stalk on;
Those great sea-horses bare their teeth and laugh at the
dawn.

J. M. SYNGE

In Glencullen

Thrush, linnet, stare, and wren,
Brown lark beside the sun,
Take thought of kestrel, sparrow-hawk,
Birdlime and roving gun.

You great-great-grandchildren
Of birds I've listened to,
I think I robbed your ancestors
When I was young as you.

The Yellow Bittern

(after the Irish of Cathal Buí Giolla Ghunna)

The yellow bittern that never broke out
   In a drinking bout, might as well have drunk;
His bones are thrown on a naked stone
   Where he lived alone like a hermit monk.
O yellow bittern! I pity your lot,
   Though they say that a sot like myself is curst –
I was sober a while, but I'll drink and be wise
   For fear I should die in the end of thirst.

It's not for the common birds that I'd mourn,
   The black-bird, the corn-crake or the crane,
But for the bittern that's shy and apart
   And drinks in the marsh from the lone bog-drain.
Oh! if I had known you were near your death,
   While my breath held out I'd have run to you,
Till a splash from the Lake of the Son of the Bird
   Your soul would have stirred and waked anew.

My darling told me to drink no more
   Or my life would be o'er in a little short while;
But I told her 'tis drink gives me health and strength
   And will lengthen my road by many a mile.
You see how the bird of the long smooth neck
   Could get his death from the thirst at last –
Come, son of my soul, and drain your cup,
   You'll get no sup when your life is past.

In a wintering island by Constantine's halls
   A bittern calls from a wineless place,
And tells me that hither he cannot come
   Till the summer is here and the sunny days.
When he crosses the stream there and wings o'er the sea
   Then a fear comes to me he may fail in his flight –
Well, the milk and the ale are drunk every drop,
   And a dram won't stop our thirst this night.

The Goat Paths

The crooked paths go every way
   Upon the hill – they wind about
Through the heather in and out
Of the quiet sunniness.
And there the goats, day after day,
   Stray in sunny quietness,
Cropping here and cropping there,
   As they pause and turn and pass,
Now a bit of heather spray,
   Now a mouthful of the grass.

In the deeper sunniness,
   In the place where nothing stirs,
Quietly in quietness,
   In the quiet of the furze,
For a time they come and lie
Staring on the roving sky.
If you approach they run away,
   They leap and stare, away they bound,
   With a sudden angry sound,
To the sunny quietude;
   Crouching down where nothing stirs
   In the silence of the furze,
Crouching down again to brood
   In the sunny solitude.

If I were as wise as they
   I would stray apart and brood,
I would beat a hidden way
Through the quiet heather spray
   To a sunny solitude;
And should you come I'd run away,
   I would make an angry sound,

I would stare and turn and bound
To the deeper quietude,
To the place where nothing stirs
In the silence of the furze.
In that airy quietness
I would think as long as they;
Through the quiet sunniness
I would stray away to brood
By a hidden beaten way
In a sunny solitude.
I would think until I found
Something I can never find,
Something lying on the ground,
In the bottom of my mind.

Ad Limina

The ewes and lambs, loving the far hillplaces,
Cropping by choice the succulent tops of heather,
Drinking the pure water of cloudborn lochlands,
Resting under erratics fostered with Abel –
Come to my haggard gate, my very doorstep.

The birds of freest will and strongest wingbeat,
Sad curlew, garrulous stonechat, hawk and coaltit,
Haunting lone bog or scalp or broken ruin,
Poising the rough thrust of air's excesses –
Come to my haggard gate, my very doorstep.

The trout in the river, below the hanging marllot,
Swift, with ancestral fear of hook and shadow,
The elvers of cold drain and slough, remembering
The warm tangles of Caribbee and Sargasso –
Come to my haggard gate, my very doorstep.

Even the stoats and rats, who know a possessor
Of the rare sixth sense, the bardic insight,
Match, and more, for their devilish perversions,
And the deer, shyest of shy at autumn rutting –
Come to my haggard gate, my very doorstep.

Am I not a lucky man, trusted, Franciscan,
That these spacious things, gentle or hostile,
Following God's urge, denying their nature,
Harbingers of high thoughts and fathers of poems –
Come to my haggard gate, my very doorstep.

PADRAIC COLUM

She Moved through the Fair

My young love said to me, 'My brothers won't mind,
And my parents won't slight you for your lack of kind.'
Then she stepped away from me, and this she did say,
'It will not be long, love, till our wedding day.'

She stepped away from me and she moved through the fair,
And fondly I watched her go here and go there,
Then she went her way homeward with one star awake,
As the swan in the evening moves over the lake.

The people were saying no two were e'er wed
But one had a sorrow that never was said,
And I smiled as she passed with her goods and her gear,
And that was the last that I saw of my dear.

I dreamt it last night that my young love came in,
So softly she entered, her feet made no din;
She came close beside me, and this she did say,
'It will not be long, love, till our wedding day.'

Tilly

He travels after a winter sun,
Urging the cattle along a cold red road,
Calling to them, a voice they know,
He drives his beasts above Cabra.

The voice tells them home is warm.
They moo and make brute music with their hoofs.
He drives them with a flowering branch before him,
Smoke pluming their foreheads.

Boor, bond of the herd,
Tonight stretch full by the fire!
I bleed by the black stream
For my torn bough!

Dublin, 1904

The Wife of Llew

And Gwydion said to Math, when it was Spring:
'Come now and let us make a wife for Llew.'
And so they broke broad boughs yet moist with dew,
And in a shadow made a magic ring:
They took the violet and the meadowsweet
To form her pretty face, and for her feet
They built a mound of daisies on a wing,
And for her voice they made a linnet sing
In the wide poppy blowing for her mouth.
And over all they chanted twenty hours.
And Llew came singing from the azure south
And bore away his wife of birds and flowers.

For France

(after the Latin of Claudian)

Even as the cattle in the winter woods,
Hearing their master's old familiar shout,
Come shouldering down to the remembered pastures
Deep in the valley, answering faithful lowing,
Each stepping in her order,
Till through the twilight of the naked branches
Glints the last straggler's horn:
So came the legions from the uttermost isles
Of Britain, where they held the Scots in leash,
And those that were a wall against the Ruhr,
And cowed the churls of Hesse and Thuringen,
They've turned the splendid menace of their line
Against the threat to Italy: they're gone.
The right bank's naked of its garrison.
Nought but the terror of the Roman name
Defends an open frontier.
To-night there is no watch upon the Rhine.

c. 1940

The Lost Heifer

When the black herds of the rain were grazing
In the gap of the pure cold wind
And the watery hazes of the hazel
Brought her into my mind,
I thought of the last honey by the water
That no hive can find.

Brightness was drenching through the branches
When she wandered again,
Turning the silver out of dark grasses
Where the skylark had lain,
And her voice coming softly over the meadow
Was the mist becoming rain.

The Planter's Daughter

When night stirred at sea
And the fire brought a crowd in,
They say that her beauty
Was music in mouth
And few in the candlelight
Thought her too proud,
For the house of the planter
Is known by the trees.

Men that had seen her
Drank deep and were silent,
The women were speaking
Wherever she went –
As a bell that is rung
Or a wonder told shyly,
And O she was the Sunday
In every week.

PATRICK MACDONOGH

Over the Water

Through weeks of this windy April with horror hawking
reason
Reiterated boasting of thrush and blackbird wakened
Anger and lonely hatred that they in their happy season
Cared less for her lost grieving than rapt unknowing faces
She scanned in brittle streets. But oh! returning soon,
Curlew and plover only were brothers to her sorrow
Crying from lonely tillage to a house of empty rooms,
They and that ragged heron who laboured up to tree-tops
Leaving reed-broken silver before her troubled movements.

May brought the south to mellow April's harsh brightness,
But brought no timid stirring of hope to my darling,
There where the wild duck convoys her young from reedy
islands
Through narrows wharfed by lilies, she saw their shadows
darken,
Cruciform on the water when foul birds from the sea
Came in for prey. But I had comfort slogging
Hard roads with marching hundreds, lulling a private grief,
Dulling in rhythmic stupor the fierce assaults of longing
And dreading memory less than lacerated feet.

Though noon will drowse in roses her young days carry
coolness
Cropped from Meath's dawning acres or stolen from
shadows
Under Dunboyne's tall hedges that lately shut the moon
From those more lucky lovers whom flitting dusk had
gathered

In gentle couples. Here skies have scarcely room
To house their clouds of bombers, yet had I but my darling,
We'd mix our hate with pity for stripling airmen doomed
To their own strange damnation, and in a night of horror
Softly we'd lie together under a bomber's moon.

Father and Son

Only last week, walking the hushed fields
Of our most lovely Meath, now thinned by November,
I came to where the road from Laracor leads
To the Boyne river – that seemed more lake than river,
Stretched in uneasy light and stript of reeds.

And walking longside an old weir
Of my people's, where nothing stirs – only the shadowed
Leaden flight of a heron up the lean air –
I went unmanly with grief, knowing how my father,
Happy though captive in years, walked last with me there.

Yes, happy in Meath with me for a day
He walked, taking stock of herds hid in their own breathing;
And naming colts, gusty as wind, once steered by his hand,
Lightnings winked in the eyes that were half shy in greeting
Old friends – the wild blades, when he gallivanted the land.

For that proud, wayward man now my heart breaks –
Breaks for that man whose mind was a secret eyrie,
Whose kind hand was sole signet of his race,
Who curbed me, scorned my green ways, yet increasingly
  loved me
Till Death drew its grey blind down his face.

And yet I am pleased that even my reckless ways
Are living shades of his rich calms and passions –
Witnesses for him and for those faint namesakes
With whom now he is one, under yew branches,
Yes, one in a graven silence no bird breaks.

FRANK O'CONNOR

Advice to Lovers

(after the Irish)

The way to get on with a girl
Is to drift like a man in a mist,
Happy enough to be caught,
Happy to be dismissed,

Glad to be out of her way,
Glad to rejoin her in bed,
Equally grieved or gay
To learn that she's living or dead.

Innocence

They laughed at one I loved –
The triangular hill that hung
Under the Big Forth. They said
That I was bounded by the whitethorn hedges
Of the little farm and did not know the world.
But I knew that love's doorway to life
Is the same doorway everywhere.

Ashamed of what I loved
I flung her from me and called her a ditch
Although she was smiling at me with violets.

But now I am back in her briary arms
The dew of an Indian Summer morning lies
On bleached potato-stalks –
What age am I?

I do not know what age I am,
I am no mortal age;
I know nothing of women,
Nothing of cities,
I cannot die
Unless I walk outside these whitethorn hedges.

Epic

I have lived in important places, times
When great events were decided: who owned
That half a rood of rock, a no-man's land
Surrounded by our pitchfork-armed claims.
I heard the Duffys shouting 'Damn your soul'
And old McCabe stripped to the waist, seen
Step the plot defying blue cast-steel –

'Here is the march along these iron stones'.
That was the year of the Munich bother. Which
Was most important? I inclined
To lose my faith in Ballyrush and Gortin
Till Homer's ghost came whispering to my mind
He said: I made the *Iliad* from such
A local row. Gods make their own importance.

In Memory of My Mother

I do not think of you lying in the wet clay
Of a Monaghan graveyard; I see
You walking down a lane among the poplars
On your way to the station, or happily

Going to second Mass on a summer Sunday.
You meet me and you say:
'Don't forget to see about the cattle –'
Among your earthiest words the angels stray.

And I think of you walking along a headland
Of green oats in June,
So full of repose, so rich with life;
And I see us meeting at the end of a town

On a fair day by accident, after
The bargains are all made and we can walk
Together through the shops and stalls and markets
Free in the oriental streets of thought.

O you are not lying in the wet clay,
For it is a harvest evening now and we
Are piling up the ricks against the moonlight
And you smile up at us – eternally.

A Flask of Brandy

You, said the Lionwoman,
Pliz, this errand, a snipe of brandy
From the first shop. Here's money;
And for you this penny.

And on my way I saw:
Item, a clown who waltzed on stilts;
A bear saluting with a paw;
Two pairs of dancing dogs in kilts;
Eight midget ponies in a single file,
A very piccolo of ponies;
Then the princess far off in her smile;
And the seven beautiful distant ladies:
And then –

Facing after the big bandwagon, he
The boy in spangles, lonely and profound:
Behind him the Ringmaster, a redfaced man,
Followed by silence heavy as a wound,
And empty.

Quickly as two feet can did I come back
To the Lionwoman with her cognac.

You, said the Lionwoman;
Pliz to the window, said foreign gutterals in
The cave of the caravan.
I waited, errand done.

And waiting on one foot saw:
Item: a twitching coloured chintz
Moved by a lemontaloned claw:
And after a woman with her face in paints,
A throat thickened in its round of tan

On shoulders sick and white with nature;
Behind was a pair of bloomers on a line,
Blue; a table with a tin platter:
More else:

A black electric cat, a stove, a pot
Purring, and a wild Red Indian blanket
Crouching sidewise on a bunk;
And some exciting smell that stunk
Till the Lionwoman rising blotted out
All but a breast as heavy as a sigh
That stared at me from one bruised eye.

JOHN HEWITT

Substance and Shadow

There is a bareness in the images
I temper time with in my mind's defence;
they hold their own, their stubborn secrecies;
no use to rage against their reticence:
a gannet's plunge, a heron by a pond,
a last rook homing as the sun goes down,
a spider squatting on a bracken-frond,
and thistles in a cornsheaf's tufted crown,
a boulder on a hillside, lichen-stained,
the sparks of sun on dripping icicles,
their durable significance contained
in texture, colour, shape, and nothing else.
All these are sharp, spare, simple, native to
this small republic I have charted out
as the sure acre where my sense is true,
while round its boundaries sprawl the screes of doubt.

My lamp lights up the kettle on the stove
and throws its shadow on the whitewashed wall,
like some Assyrian profile with, above,
a snake, or bird-prowed helmet crested tall;
but this remains a shadow; when I shift
the lamp or move the kettle it is gone,
the substance and the shadow break adrift
that needed bronze to lock them, bronze or stone.

A Local Poet

He followed their lilting stanzas
through a thousand columns or more,
and scratched for the splintered couplets
in the cracks on the cottage floor,
for his Rhyming Weavers fell silent
when they flocked through the factory door.

He'd imagined a highway of heroes
and stepped aside on the grass
to let Cuchullain's chariot through,
and the Starry Ploughmen pass;
but he met the Travelling Gunman
instead of the Galloglass.

And so, with luck, for a decade
down the widowed years ahead,
the pension which crippled his courage
will keep him in daily bread,
while he mourns for his mannerly verses
that had left so much unsaid.

Roundelay

on all that strand
at end of day
steps sole sound
long sole sound
until unbidden stay
then no sound
on all that strand
long no sound
until unbidden go
steps sole sound
long sole sound
on all that strand
at end of day

Mayfly

Barometer of my moods today, mayfly,
Up and down one among a million, one
The same at best as the rest of the jigging mayflies,
One only day of May alive beneath the sun.

The yokels tilt their pewters and the foam
Flowers in the sun beside the jewelled water.
Daughter of the South, call the sunbeams home
To nest between your breasts. The kingcups
Ephemeral are gay gulps of laughter.

Gulp of yellow merriment; cackle of ripples;
Lips of the river that pout and whisper round the reeds.
The mayfly flirting and posturing over the water
Goes up and down in the lift so many times for fun.

'When we are grown up we are sure to alter
Much for the better, to adopt solider creeds;
The kingcup will cease proffering his cup
And the foam will have blown from the beer and the heat no
  longer dance
And the lift lose fascination and the May
Change her tune to June – but the trouble with us mayflies
Is that we never have the chance to be grown up.'

They never have the chance, but what of time they have
They stretch out taut and thin and ringing clear;
So we, whose strand of life is not much more,
Let us too make our time elastic and
Inconsequently dance above the dazzling wave.

Nor put too much on the sympathy of things,
The dregs of drink, the dried cups of flowers,
The pathetic fallacy of the passing hours

When it is we who pass them – hours of stone,
Long rows of granite sphinxes looking on.

It is we who pass them, we the circus masters
Who make the mayflies dance, the lapwings lift their crests;
The show will soon shut down, its gay-rags gone,
But when this summer is over let us die together,
I want always to be near your breasts.

Brother Fire

When our brother Fire was having his dog's day
Jumping the London streets with millions of tin cans
Clanking at his tail, we heard some shadow say
'Give the dog a bone' – and so we gave him ours;
Night after night we watched him slaver and crunch away
The beams of human life, the tops of topless towers.

Which gluttony of his for us was Lenten fare
Who mother-naked, suckled with sparks, were chill
Though cotted in a grille of sizzling air
Striped like a convict – black, yellow and red;
Thus were we weaned to knowledge of the Will
That wills the natural world but wills us dead.

O delicate walker, babbler, dialectician Fire,
O enemy and image of ourselves,
Did we not on those mornings after the All Clear,
When you were looting shops in elemental joy
And singing as you swarmed up city block and spire,
Echo your thoughts in ours? 'Destroy! Destroy!'

Charon

The conductor's hands were black with money:
Hold on to your ticket, he said, the inspector's
Mind is black with suspicion, and hold on to
That dissolving map. We moved through London,
We could see the pigeons through the glass but failed
To hear their rumours of wars, we could see
The lost dog barking but never knew
That his bark was as shrill as a cock crowing,
We just jogged on, at each request
Stop there was a crowd of aggressively vacant
Faces, we just jogged on, eternity
Gave itself airs in revolving lights
And then we came to the Thames and all
The bridges were down, the further shore
Was lost in fog, so we asked the conductor
What we should do. He said: Take the ferry
Faute de mieux. We flicked the flashlight
And there was the ferryman just as Virgil
And Dante had seen him. He looked at us coldly
And his eyes were dead and his hands on the oar
Were black with obols and varicose veins
Marbled his calves and he said to us coldly:
If you want to die you will have to pay for it.

Glór Acastóra

Cá bhfuilir uaim le fada
A ghlór acastóra?
Thiar i gcúl an ama atáir
Cé gur iomaí oíche i bhfad ó shin
Ba cheol tú i mo chluasa.

Carr Aindí Goill ar chapall maith
Bhíodh ag dul in aghaidh aird
Ar a bhealach go hEoghanacht.
Deireann súile m'aigne liom
Go raibh péint ghlé dhearg air,
Ach ní hé sin is measa liom
Ná is mó a airím uaim,
Ach glór an acastóra
A bhogadh chun suain mé.

Axle Song

Where have you been this long time,
Song of the axle?
Hidden in time's backyard
Though many a night long ago
You were music to my ears.

Andy Goill's cart behind a good horse
Was climbing the slope
On the way to Ownaght.
My mind's eye tells me
It was painted bright red,
But that's not my keenest memory
Nor what I miss the most,
But the song of the axle
That lulled me to sleep.

translated by Tomás Mac Síomóin and Douglas Sealy

Field Day

The old farmer, nearing death, asked
To be carried outside and set down
Where he could see a certain field
'And then I will cry my heart out,' he said.

It troubles me, thinking about that man;
What shape was the field of his crying
In Donegal?

I remember a small field in Down, a field
Within fields, shaped like a triangle.
I could have stood there and looked at it
All day long.

And I remember crossing the frontier between
France and Spain at a forbidden point, and seeing
A small triangular field in Spain,
And stopping

Or walking in Ireland down any rutted by-road
To where it hit the highway, there was always
At this turning-point and abutment
A still centre, a V-shape of grass
Untouched by cornering traffic,
Where country lads larked at night.

I think I know what the shape of the field was
That made the old man weep.

DONAGH MACDONAGH

Just an Old Sweet Song

The pale, drooping girl and the swaggering soldier,
The row-dow-dow-dow of the stuttering drum,
The bugles, the charges, the swords are romantic
For those who survive when the bugles are dumb.

The lice of the trenches, the mortars, machine-guns,
The prisoners exchanged and the Christmas Day lull,
The no-man's-land raid and the swagger-stick rally
Are stirring, for when was a finished war dull?

The road-block, the ambush, the scrap on the mountain,
The slouch-hat, the trench-coat, the raid in the night,
The hand-grenade hefted, police-barracks burning
Ah, that was the life, and who's hurt in a fight?

The blitzkrieg, the landings, the victories, the losses,
The eyes blind with sand, the retreat, the alert,
Commando and D-Day, H-Hour and Block-buster
Have filed through the glass, and was anyone hurt?

A flash and a mushroom, a hole in the planet,
Strange growth in the flora, less fauna to feed.
Peace enters, the silence returns and the waters
Advance on the earth as the war tides recede.

Malairt

'Gaibh i leith,' arsa Turnbull, 'go bhfeice tú an brón
  I súilibh an chapaill,
Dá mbeadh crúba chomh mór leo sin fútsa bheadh brón
  Id shúilibh chomh maith leis.'

Agus b'fhollas gur thuig sé chomh maith sin an brón
  I súilibh an chapaill,
Is gur mhachnaigh chomh cruaidh air gur tomadh é fá
    dheoidh
  In aigne an chapaill.

D'fhéachas ar an gcapall go bhfeicinn an brón
  'Na shúilibh ag seasamh,
Do chonac súile Turnbull ag féachaint im threo
  As cloigeann an chapaill.

D'fhéachas ar Turnbull is d'fhéachas air fá dhó
  Is do chonac ar a leacain
Na súile rómhóra bhí balbh le brón –
  Súile an chapaill.

Mirror

‘Come over here’, said Turnbull, ‘till you see the sorrow
 In the horse’s eyes.
If you had hooves as cumbersome, there would be gloom
 In your eyes too.’

And it struck me that he’d so realised the sorrow
 In the horse’s eyes,
So deeply had he contemplated it, that he’d been steeped
 In the horse’s mind.

I looked at the horse, that I might see the sorrow
 Looming in its eyes,
And saw instead the eyes of Turnbull peering at me
 From the horse’s head.

I looked at Turnbull, then took a second look,
 And saw beneath his brows
The over-big eyes that were dumb with sorrow –
 The horse’s eyes.

translated by Ciaran Carson

Reo

Maidin sheaca ghabhas amach
Is bhí seál póca romham ar sceach,
Rugas air le cur im phóca
Ach sciorr sé uaim mar bhí sé reoite:
Ní héadach beo a léim óm ghlaic
Ach rud fuair bás aréir ar sceach:
Is siúd ag taighde mé fé m'intinn
Go bhfuaireas macasamhail an ní seo –
  Lá dar phógas bean dem mhuintir
  Is í ina cónra reoite, sínte.

Frost

I found a hankie on the whitethorn
outside in the freezing cold this morning.
When I reached up to get it, it slipped –
or skipped? Anyhow it missed my grip.
Not just a sprightly rag, I thought,
more like 'something' died out here last night ...
As I sought the right analogy
this surfaced in my memory:
  The kiss I gave my cousin
  before they covered her coffin.

translated by Maurice Riordan

VALENTIN IREMONGER

The Toy Horse

Somebody, when I was young, stole my toy horse,
The charm of my morning romps, my man's delight.
For two days I grieved, holding my sorrow like flowers
Between the bars of my sullen angry mind.

Next day I went out with evil in my heart,
Evil between my eyes and at the tips of my hands,
Looking for my enemy at the armed stations,
Until I found him, playing in his garden

With my toy horse, urgent in the battle
Against the enemies of his Unreason's land:
He was so happy, I gave him also
My vivid coloured crayons and my big glass marble.

Portrait of a Woman from the Fayum

The painter of mummy portraits came today
And spoke to father about my symptoms.
Overhearing words like 'mortal illness',
I was not surprised, given how I feel.
A girl, they call me, but I look years older,
My skin the colour of papyrus, brown eyes
Facing other eyes with open-ended questions
And a mind that gloats over the present,
Having no wish to be other-worldly.

When he comes to make a sketch from the life,
With his paints, brushes, charcoal stove and wax,
I shall put on my emeralds and garnets,
Small though they are, as well as my gold ball earrings,
With an understated Roman-style fringe
Above my forehead and enquiring eyebrows.
And I shall ask my mother to dress my body
In that fine peplum (with the purple border),
When the real me has embarked for the underworld.

I've not been specially good, but I've tried
Not to scandalize the impartial gods.
Forgive me, self-pity is wrong, I know,
But tears seem to have a will of their own.
Through the doorway I can see the bulrushes
Swaying in the wind off the Libyan desert
And hear the teal burbling on Lake Moeris,
While down the road the light-hearted village women
Ululate at someone else's wedding feast.

Athdheirdre

'Ní bhearrfad m'ingne,'
Adúirt sí siúd
Is do thug cúl don saol
De dheascaibh an aonlae sin –
Lena cré
Ní mhaífinnse,
Ná mo leithéidse, gaol –
   Cíoraim mo cheann
   Is cuirim dath fém bhéal.

A Second Deirdre

'I'll not cut my nails,'
That first one said,
And turned her back on life
That very day –
With the like of her
I'd claim no more kinship
Than any of my sort –
   I comb my hair,
   I lipstick my lips.

translated by Patrick Crotty

The British Connection

In Belfast, Europe, your man
Met the Military come to raid
The house:
              'Over my dead body
Sir,' he said, brandishing
A real-life sword from some
Old half-forgotten war . . .

And youths with real bows and arrows
And coppers and marbles good as bullets
And oldtime thrupenny bits and stones
Screws, bolts, nuts (Belfast confetti),

And kitchen knives, pokers, Guinness tins
And nail-bombs down by the Shore Road

And guns under the harbour wharf
And bullets in the docker's tea tin
And gelignite in the tool shed
And grenades in the scullery larder
And weedkiller and sugar
And acid in the french letter

And sodium chlorate and nitrates
In the suburban garage
In the boot of the car

And guns in the oven grill
And guns in the spinster's shift

And ammunition and more more
Guns in the broken-down rusted
Merry-Go-Round in the Scrap Yard

Almost as many hard-on
Guns as there are union jacks.

Stormpetrel

Gipsy of the sea
In winter wambling over scurvy whaleroads,
Jooking in the wake of ships,
A sailor hooks you
And carves his girl's name on your beak.

Guest of the storm
Who sweeps you off to party after party,
You flit in a sooty grey coat
Smelling of must
Barefoot across a sea of broken glass.

Waif of the afterglow
On summer nights to meet your mate you jink
Over sea-cliff and graveyard,
Creeping underground
To hatch an egg in a hermit's skull.

Pulse of the rock
You throb till daybreak on your cryptic nest
A song older than fossils,
Ephemeral as thrift.
It ends with a gasp.

Sunup

The sun kisses my eyes open:
Another day of wanting you.
I'd like to kiss your eyes again,
No comfort now in being alone.

Is she delighting you in bed
In her caravan on a cutaway road?
Does the sun give you the same kiss
To wake you, with her at your side?

I kiss you both, like the sun,
I kiss your hands and your feet,
Your ears and your eyes,
Both your bodies, I bless them both.

Do you feel this when you make love?
Do you love her as I loved you?
Will you let her steal all you have
And suffer her to leave?

Meet me today! We'll find a wood
Of blackthorn in white bud:
And let me give you one more kiss
Full of sun, free of bitterness.

PEARSE HUTCHINSON

Into Their True Gentleness

for Katherine Kavanagh

If love is the greatest reality,
and I believe it is,
the gentle are more real
than the violent or than
those like me who
hate violence,
long for gentleness,
but never in our own act
achieve true gentleness.
We fall in love with people
we consider gentle,
we love them violently
for their gentleness,
so violently we drive
them to violence,
for our gentleness
is less real
than their breaking patience,
so falsely we accuse
them of being false.

But with any luck,
time half-opens our eyes
to at least a hundredth
part of our absurdity,
and lets them travel back,
released from us,
into their true gentleness,
even with us.

THOMAS KINSELLA

Hen Woman

The noon heat in the yard
smelled of stillness and coming thunder.
A hen scratched and picked at the shore.
It stopped, its body crouched and puffed out.
The brooding silence seemed to say 'Hush ...'

The cottage door opened,
a black hole
in a whitewashed wall so bright
the eyes narrowed.
Inside, a clock murmured 'Gong ...'

(I had felt all this before ...)

She hurried out in her slippers
muttering, her face dark with anger,
and gathered the hen up jerking
languidly. Her hand fumbled.
Too late. Too late.

It fixed me with its pebble eyes
(seeing what mad blur?).
A white egg showed in the sphincter;
mouth and beak opened together;
and time stood still.

Nothing moved; bird or woman,
fumbled or fumbling – locked there
(as I must have been) gaping.

*

There was a tiny movement at my feet,
tiny and mechanical; I looked down.
A beetle like a bronze leaf

was inching across the cement,
clasping with small tarsi
a ball of dung bigger than its body.
The serrated brow pressed the ground humbly,
lifted in a short stare, bowed again;
the dung-ball advanced minutely,
losing a few fragments,
specks of staleness and freshness.

*

A mutter of thunder far off
– time not quite stopped.
I saw the egg had moved a fraction:
a tender blank brain
under torsion, a clean new world.

As I watched, the mystery completed.
The black zero of the orifice
closed to a point
and the white zero of the egg hung free,
flecked with greenish brown oils.

It slowly turned and fell.
Dreamlike, fussed by her splayed fingers,
it floated outward, moon-white,
leaving no trace in the air,
and began its drop to the shore.

*

I feed upon it still, as you see;
there is no end to that which,
not understood, may yet be noted
and hoarded in the imagination,
in the yolk of one's being, so to speak,
there to undergo its (quite animal) growth,
dividing blindly,
twitching, packed with will,

searching in its own tissue
for the structure
in which it may wake.
Something that had – clenched
in its cave – not been
now was: an egg of being.
Through what seemed a whole year it fell
– as it still falls, for me,
solid and light, the red gold beating
in its silvery womb,
alive as the yolk and white
of my eye; as it will continue
to fall, probably, until I die,
through the vast indifferent spaces
with which I am empty.

*

It smashed against the grating
and slipped down quickly out of sight.
It was over in a comical flash.
The soft mucous shell clung a little longer,
then drained down.
She stood staring, in blank anger.
Then her eyes came to life, and she laughed
and let the bird flap away.
'It's all the one.
There's plenty more where that came from!'

Hen to pan!
It was a simple world.

Wyncote, Pennsylvania: A Gloss

A mocking-bird on a branch
outside the window, where I write,
gulps down a wet crimson berry,
shakes off a few bright drops
from his wing, and is gone
into a thundery sky.

Another storm coming.
Under that copper light
my papers seem luminous.
And over them I will take
ever more painstaking care.

JOHN MONTAGUE

All Legendary Obstacles

All legendary obstacles lay between
Us, the long imaginary plain,
The monstrous ruck of mountains
And, swinging across the night,
Flooding the Sacramento, San Joaquin,
The hissing drift of winter rain.

All day I waited, shifting
Nervously from station to bar
As I saw another train sail
By, the San Francisco Chief or
Golden Gate, water dripping
From great flanged wheels.

At midnight you came, pale
Above the negro porter's lamp.
I was too blind with rain
And doubt to speak, but
Reached from the platform
Until our chilled hands met.

You had been travelling for days
With an old lady, who marked
A neat circle on the glass
With her glove, to watch us
Move into the wet darkness
Kissing, still unable to speak.

A Bright Day

for John McGahern

At times I see it, present
   As a bright day, or a hill,
The only way of saying something
   Luminously as possible.

Not the accumulated richness
   Of an old historical language –
That musk-deep odour!
   But a slow exactness

Which recreates experience
   By ritualizing its details –
Pale web of curtain, width
   Of deal table, till all

Takes on a witch-bright glow
   And even the clock on the mantel
Moves its hands in a fierce delight
   Of so, and so, and so.

TOM MACINTYRE

Kisses

Would you like to hear
of the kisses we share?

Track of The Sanderlings,
Hide-and-Seek of The Swallow,
Yellow-Hammer-And-Tongs,

Tit's Morning Milk,
Linnet Reflecting, Sweet
Sleep of The Thrush,

Swift Going South, Take
Your Fill of The Thermal,
Streak of The Kingfisher,
Golden Plovers Wheel The Shore –

nights like tonight,
Lord, how they play,
as The Summer Triangle
folds The Milky Way.

Bread

Someone else cut off my head
In a golden field.
Now I am re-created

By her fingers. This
Moulding is more delicate
Than a first kiss,

More deliberate than her own
Rising up
And lying down.

Even at my weakest, I am
Finer than anything
In this legendary garden

Yet I am nothing till
She runs her fingers through me
And shapes me with her skill.

The form that I shall bear
Grows round and white.
It seems I comfort her

Even as she slits my face
And stabs my chest.
Her feeling for perfection is

Absolute.
So I am glad to go through fire
And come out

Shaped like her dream.
In my way
I am all that can happen to men.
I came to life at her fingerends.
I will go back into her again.

From the Irish

Most terrible was our hero in battle blows:
hands without fingers, shorn heads and toes
were scattered. That day there flew and fell
from astonished victims eyebrow, bone and entrail,
like stars in the sky, like snowflakes, like nuts in May,
like a meadow of daisies, like butts from an ashtray.

Familiar things, you might brush against or tread
upon in the daily round, were glistening red
with the slaughter the hero caused, though he had gone.
By proxy his bomb exploded, his valour shone.

MICHAEL COADY

Letting Go

I love the abandon
of abandoned things

the harmonium surrendering
in a churchyard in Aherlow,
the hearse resigned to nettles
behind a pub in Carna,
the tin dancehall possessed
by convolvulus in Kerry,
the living room that hosts
a tree in south Kilkenny.

I sense a rapture
in deserted things

washed-out circus posters
derelict on gables,
lush forgotten sidings
of country railway stations,
bat droppings profligate
on pew and font and lectern,
the wedding dress a dog
has nosed from a dustbin.

I love the openness
of things no longer viable,
I sense their shameless
slow unbuttoning:
the implicit nakedness
there for the taking,
the surrender to the dance
of breaking and creating.

Mossbawn: Sunlight

There was a sunlit absence.
The helmeted pump in the yard
heated its iron,
water honeyed

in the slung bucket
and the sun stood
like a griddle cooling
against the wall

of each long afternoon.
So, her hands scuffled
over the bakeboard,
the reddening stove

sent its plaque of heat
against her where she stood
in a floury apron
by the window.

Now she dusts the board
with a goose's wing,
now sits, broad-lapped,
with whitened nails

and measling shins:
here is a space
again, the scone rising
to the tick of two clocks.

And here is love
like a tinsmith's scoop
sunk past its gleam
in the meal-bin.

Casualty

1

He would drink by himself
And raise a weathered thumb
Towards the high shelf,
Calling another rum
And blackcurrant, without
Having to raise his voice,
Or order a quick stout
By a lifting of the eyes
And a discreet dumb-show
Of pulling off the top;
At closing time would go
In waders and peaked cap
Into the showery dark,
A dole-kept breadwinner
But a natural for work.
I loved his whole manner,
Sure-footed but too sly,
His deadpan sidling tact,
His fisherman's quick eye
And turned observant back.

Incomprehensible
To him, my other life.
Sometimes, on his high stool,
Too busy with his knife
At a tobacco plug
And not meeting my eye,
In the pause after a slug
He mentioned poetry.
We would be on our own
And, always politic

And shy of condescension,
I would manage by some trick
To switch the talk to eels
Or lore of the horse and cart
Or the Provisionals.

But my tentative art
His turned back watches too:
He was blown to bits
Out drinking in a curfew
Others obeyed, three nights
After they shot dead
The thirteen men in Derry.
PARAS THIRTEEN, the walls said,
BOGSIDE NIL. That Wednesday
Everybody held
His breath and trembled.

2

It was a day of cold
Raw silence, wind-blown
Surplice and soutane:
Rained-on, flower-laden
Coffin after coffin
Seemed to float from the door
Of the packed cathedral
Like blossoms on slow water.
The common funeral
Unrolled its swaddling band,
Lapping, tightening
Till we were braced and bound
Like brothers in a ring.

But he would not be held
At home by his own crowd
Whatever threats were phoned,

Whatever black flags waved.
I see him as he turned
In that bombed offending place,
Remorse fused with terror
In his still knowable face,
His cornered outfaced stare
Blinding in the flash.

He had gone miles away
For he drank like a fish
Nightly, naturally
Swimming towards the lure
Of warm lit-up places,
The blurred mesh and murmur
Drifting among glasses
In the gregarious smoke.
How culpable was he
That last night when he broke
Our tribe's complicity?
'Now you're supposed to be
An educated man,'
I hear him say, 'Puzzle me
The right answer to that one.'

3

I missed his funeral,
Those quiet walkers
And sideways talkers
Shoaling out of his lane
To the respectable
Purring of the hearse . . .
They move in equal pace
With the habitual
Slow consolation
Of a dawdling engine,
The line lifted, hand

Over first, cold sunshine
On the water, the land
Banked under fog: that morning
I was taken in his boat,
The screw purling, turning
Indolent fathoms white,
I tasted freedom with him.
To get out early, haul
Steadily off the bottom,
Dispraise the catch, and smile
As you find a rhythm
Working you, slow mile by mile,
Into your proper haunt
Somewhere, well out, beyond . . .

Dawn-sniffing revenant,
Plodder through midnight rain,
Question me again.

The Harvest Bow

As you plaited the harvest bow
You implicated the mellowed silence in you
In wheat that does not rust
But brightens as it tightens twist by twist
Into a knowable corona,
A throwaway love-knot of straw.

Hands that aged round ashplants and cane sticks
And lapped the spurs on a lifetime of game cocks
Harked to their gift and worked with fine intent
Until your fingers moved somnambulant:
I tell and finger it like braille,
Gleaning the unsaid off the palpable,

And if I spy into its golden loops
I see us walk between the railway slopes
Into an evening of long grass and midges,
Blue smoke straight up, old beds and ploughs in hedges,
An auction notice on an outhouse wall –
You with a harvest bow in your lapel,

Me with the fishing rod, already homesick
For the big lift of these evenings, as your stick
Whacking the tips off weeds and bushes
Beats out of time, and beats, but flushes
Nothing: that original townland
Still tongue-tied in the straw tied by your hand.

The end of art is peace
Could be the motto of this frail device
That I have pinned up on our deal dresser –
Like a drawn snare
Slipped lately by the spirit of the corn
Yet burnished by its passage, and still warm.

An Dobharchú Gonta

Dobharchú gonta
ar charraig lom
ga ina taobh,
í ag cuimilt a féasóige
ag cuimilt scamaill a cos.

Chuala sí uair
óna sinsir
go raibh abhainn ann,
abhainn chriostail,
gan uisce inti.

Chuala fós go raibh breac ann
chomh ramhar le stoc crainn,
go raibh cruidín ann
mar gha geal gorm;
chuala fós go raibh fear ann
gan luaith ina bhróga,
go raibh fear ann
gan chúnna ar chordaí.

D'éag an domhan,
d'éag an ghrian i ngan fhios di
mar bhí sí cheana
ag snámh go sámh
in abhainn dhraíochta an chriostail.

The Wounded Otter

A wounded otter
on a bare rock
a bolt in her side,
stroking her whiskers
stroking her webbed feet.

Her ancestors
told her once
that there was a river,
a crystal river,
a waterless bed.

They also said
there were trout there
fat as tree-trunks
and kingfishers
bright as blue spears –
men there without cinders
in their boots,
men without dogs
on leashes.

She did not notice
the world die
nor the sun expire.
She was already
swimming at ease
in the magic crystal river.

translated by the author

Death of an Irishwoman

Ignorant, in the sense
she ate monotonous food
and thought the world was flat,
and pagan, in the sense
she knew the things that moved
all night were neither dogs nor cats
but púcas and darkfaced men
she nevertheless had fierce pride.
But sentenced in the end
to eat thin diminishing porridge
in a stone-cold kitchen
she clenched her brittle hands
around a world
she could not understand.
I loved her from the day she died.
She was a summer dance at the crossroads.
She was a cardgame where a nose was broken.
She was a song that nobody sings.
She was a house ransacked by soldiers.
She was a language seldom spoken.
She was a child's purse, full of useless things.

EAMON GRENNAN

Women Going

You know the ordinary ways they go
from you and from the stark daylight
staring through an open door. This girl
leans her lips to the beak of a dove
she holds against her heart as if
insinuating the best way out and back
and whispering, *Now I have to go.*

On a stone doorpost the young wife
arches her stopped body, one hand
flat across her belly, the other
raised to straighten the seamless veil
through which the full moons of her earrings
just appear, signalling a change of state
and no way back to the here and now
of things, to the honeysuckle open air
she's been breathing. The lady of the house

holds up one necklace after another
chosen from the jewel box a servant offers
and eyes the way it might belong
between the jut of her neckbone
and where her breasts begin, fitting her
for the road that opens ahead now
and night falling: *This one,* she says
at last, picking the pearls with a clasp
curved like a wishbone. And now

across the busy street you see a man
lean into the back of a taxi
where a woman's face is barely visible
looking back into his face and not flinching
as they dispossess each other into absence

and the door in that black cloud closes over
whatever they say above the roar
of rush-hour traffic. He bends away,

and you know when he looks again
she'll be gone, and in her place will be
this absence beating its stone wings
over every ordinary corner of the day
she's left, and left him in.

The Studio

You would think with so much going on outside
The deal table would make for the window,
The ranged crockery freak and wail
Remembering its dark origins, the frail
Oil-cloth, in a fury of recognitions,
Disperse in a thousand directions
And the simple bulb in the ceiling, honed
By death to a worm of pain, to a hair
Of heat, to a light snowflake laid
On a dark river at night – and wearied
Above all by the life-price of time
And the failure by only a few tenths
Of an inch but completely and for ever
Of the ends of a carefully drawn equator
To meet, sing and be one – abruptly
Roar into the floor.
                                        But it
Never happens like that. Instead
There is this quivering silence
In which, day by day, the play
Of light and shadow (shadow mostly)
Repeats itself, though never exactly.

This is the all-purpose bed-, work- and bedroom.
Its mourning faces are cracked porcelain only quicker,
Its knuckles doorknobs only lighter,
Its occasional cries of despair
A function of the furniture.

A Disused Shed in Co. Wexford

Let them not forget us, the weak souls among the asphodels.
–Seferis, *Mythistorema*

(for J. G. Farrell)

Even now there are places where a thought might grow –
Peruvian mines, worked out and abandoned
To a slow clock of condensation,
An echo trapped for ever, and a flutter
Of wild flowers in the lift-shaft,
Indian compounds where the wind dances
And a door bangs with diminished confidence,
Lime crevices behind rippling rain-barrels,
Dog corners for bone burials;
And in a disused shed in Co. Wexford,

Deep in the grounds of a burnt-out hotel,
Among the bathtubs and the washbasins
A thousand mushrooms crowd to a keyhole.
This is the one star in their firmament
Or frames a star within a star.
What should they do there but desire?
So many days beyond the rhododendrons
With the world waltzing in its bowl of cloud,
They have learnt patience and silence
Listening to the rooks querulous in the high wood.

They have been waiting for us in a foetor
Of vegetable sweat since civil war days,
Since the gravel-crunching, interminable departure
Of the expropriated mycologist.
He never came back, and light since then
Is a keyhole rusting gently after rain.
Spiders have spun, flies dusted to mildew
And once a day, perhaps, they have heard something –

A trickle of masonry, a shout from the blue
Or a lorry changing gear at the end of the lane.

There have been deaths, the pale flesh flaking
Into the earth that nourished it;
And nightmares, born of these and the grim
Dominion of stale air and rank moisture.
Those nearest the door grow strong –
'Elbow room! Elbow room!'
The rest, dim in a twilight of crumbling
Utensils and broken flower-pots, groaning
For their deliverance, have been so long
Expectant that there is left only the posture.

A half century, without visitors, in the dark –
Poor preparation for the cracking lock
And creak of hinges. Magi, moonmen,
Powdery prisoners of the old regime,
Web-throated, stalked like triffids, racked by drought
And insomnia, only the ghost of a scream
At the flash-bulb firing-squad we wake them with
Shows there is life yet in their feverish forms.
Grown beyond nature now, soft food for worms,
They lift frail heads in gravity and good faith.

They are begging us, you see, in their wordless way,
To do something, to speak on their behalf
Or at least not to close the door again.
Lost people of Treblinka and Pompeii!
'Save us, save us,' they seem to say,
'Let the god not abandon us
Who have come so far in darkness and in pain.
We too had our lives to live.
You with your light meter and relaxed itinerary,
Let not our naive labours have been in vain!'

Tractatus

(for Aidan and Alannah)

'The world is everything that is the case'
From the fly giving up in the coal-shed
To the Winged Victory of Samothrace.
Give blame, praise, to the fumbling God
Who hides, shame-facèdly, His agèd face;
Whose light retires behind its veil of cloud.

The world, though, is also so much more –
Everything that is the case imaginatively.
Tacitus believed mariners could *hear*
The sun sinking into the western sea;
And who would question that titanic roar,
The steam rising wherever the edge may be?

EAVAN BOLAND

The Black Lace Fan My Mother Gave Me

It was the first gift he ever gave her,
buying it for five francs in the Galeries
in prewar Paris. It was stifling.
A starless drought made the nights stormy.

They stayed in the city for the summer.
They met in cafés. She was always early.
He was late. That evening he was later.
They wrapped the fan. He looked at his watch.

She looked down the Boulevard des Capucines.
She ordered more coffee. She stood up.
The streets were emptying. The heat was killing.
She thought the distance smelled of rain and lightning.

These are wild roses, appliquéd in silk
by hand – darkly picked, stitched boldly, quickly.
The rest is tortoiseshell and has the reticent,
clear patience of its element. It is

a worn-out, underwater bullion and it keeps,
even now, an inference of its violation.
The lace is overcast, as if the weather
it opened for and offset had entered it.

The past is an empty café terrace.
An airless dusk before thunder. A man running.
And no way now to know what happened then –
none at all – unless, of course, you improvise:

The blackbird on this first sultry morning
in summer, finding buds, worms, fruit,
feels the heat. Suddenly, she puts out her wing –
the whole, full, flirtatious span of it.

Fireman's Lift

I was standing beside you looking up
Through the big tree of the cupola
Where the church splits wide open to admit
Celestial choirs, the fall-out of brightness.

The Virgin was spiralling to heaven,
Hauled up in stages. Past mist and shining,
Teams of angelic arms were heaving,
Supporting, crowding her, and we stepped

Back, as the painter longed to
While his arm swept in the large strokes.
We saw the work entire, and how the light

Melted and faded bodies so that
Loose feet and elbows and staring eyes
Floated in the wide stone petticoat
Clear and free as weeds.

This is what love sees, that angle:
The crick in the branch loaded with fruit,
A jaw defining itself, a shoulder yoked,

The back making itself a roof
The legs a bridge, the hands
A crane and a cradle.

Their heads bowed over to reflect on her
Fair face and hair so like their own
As she passed through their hands. We saw them
Lifting her, the pillars of their arms

(Her face a capital leaning into an arch)
As the muscles clung and shifted
For a final purchase together
Under her weight as she came to the edge of the cloud.

Parma 1963 – Dublin 1994

Studying the Language

On Sundays I watch the hermits coming out of their holes
Into the light. Their cliff is as full as a hive.
They crowd together on warm shoulders of rock
Where the sun has been shining, their joints crackle.
They begin to talk after a while.
I listen to their accents, they are not all
From this island, not all old,
Not even, I think, all masculine.

They are so wise, they do not pretend to see me.
They drink from the scattered pools of melted snow:
I walk right by them and drink when they have done.
I can see the marks of chains around their feet.

I call this my work, these decades and stations –
Because, without these, I would be a stranger here.

In Memory: The Miami Showband: Massacred 31 July 1975

Beautiful are the feet of them that preach the gospel of peace,
Of them that bring glad tidings of good things

In a public house, darkly-lit, a patriotic (sic)
Versifier whines into my face: 'You must take one side
Or the other, or you're but a fucking romantic.'
His eyes glitter hate and vanity, porter and whiskey,
And I realise that he is blind to the braille connection
Between a music and a music-maker.
'You must take one side or the other
Or you're but a fucking romantic':
The whine is icy
And his eyes hang loose like sheets from poles
On a bare wet hillside in winter
And his mouth gapes like a cave in ice;
It is a whine in the crotch of whose fear
Is fondled a dream-gun blood-smeared;
It is in war – not poetry or music –
That men find their niche, their glory hole;
Like most of his fellows
He will abide no contradiction in the mind:
He whines: 'If there is birth, there cannot be death'
And – jabbing a hysterical forefinger into my nose and eyes –
'If there is death, there cannot be birth.'
Peace to the souls of those who unlike my confrère
Were true to their trade
Despite death-dealing blackmail by racists:
You made music, and that was all: You were realists
And beautiful were your feet.

Birth of a Coachman

His father and grandfather before him were coachmen:
How strange, then, to think that this small, bloody, lump of
flesh,
This tiny moneybags of brains, veins, and intestines,
This zipped-up purse of most peculiar coin,
Will one day be coachman of the Cork to Dublin route,
In a great black greatcoat and white gauntlets,
In full command of one of our famous coaches
– *Wonder, Perseverance, Diligence,* or *Lightning* –
In charge of all our lives on foul winter nights,
Crackling his whip, whirling it, lashing it,
Driving on the hapless horses across the moors
Of the Kilworth hills, beating them on
Across rivers in spate, rounding sharp bends
On only two wheels, shriekings of axle-trees,
Rock-scrapes, rut-squeals, quagmire-squelches,
For ever in dread of the pitiless highwayman
Lurking in ambush with a brace of pistols;
Then cantering carefully in the lee of the Galtees,
Bowing his head to the stone gods of Cashel;
Then again thrusting through Urlingford;
Doing his bit, and his nut, past the Devilsbit;
Praising the breasts of the hills round Port Laoise;
Sailing full furrow through the Curragh of Kildare,
Through the thousand sea-daisies of a thousand white sheep;
Thrashing gaily the air at first glimpse of the Liffey;
Until stepping down from his high perch in Dublin
Into the sanctuary of a cobbled courtyard,
Into the arms of a crowd like a triumphant toreador
All sweat and tears: the man of the moment
Who now is but a small body of but some fleeting seconds
old.

The Hay-Carrier

(after Veronica Bolay)

Have you ever saved hay in Mayo in the rain?
Have you ever made hay in Mayo in the sun?
Have you ever carried above your head a haycock on a
  pitchfork?
Have you ever slept in a haybarn on the road from Mayo
  into Egypt?
I am a hay-carrier.
My father was a hay-carrier.
My mother was a hay-carrier.
My brothers were hay-carriers.
My sisters were hay-carriers.
My wife is a hay-carrier.
My son is a hay-carrier.
His sons are hay-carriers.
His daughters are hay-carriers.
We were always all hay-carriers.
We will always be hay-carriers.
For the great gate of night stands painted red –
And all of heaven lies waiting to be fed.

JOHN ENNIS

A Drink of Spring

After the sweat of swathes and the sinking madder sun
The clean-raked fields of a polychrome twilight
With cloudlets of indigo nomadic on the sky,
'A drink of spring' was my father's preface to the night.

As the youngest, I made fast the dairy-window reins,
Sent the galvanized bucket plummeting to sink first
Time, weighted with steel washers at one frost-patterned side.
His request was as habitual as a creaking kitchen joist.

The rope tautened for the upward pull under the damson
Tree and back-biting thorns of a never-pruned rose.
The water, laced with lime, was glacial to the dusty throat.
Mirage of the dying, it brings relief to the lips of the comatose.

Cups furred with cold I handed round the open-door fireless
Kitchen. The taste on my lips was lingering like a first kiss.

Casement on Banna

In this dawn waking, he is Oisin
Stretching down for the boulder
That will break his girth and plunge
Him into age; he's Columcille
Waiting for foreign soil to leak
From his sandals and bring him death
In Ireland. He can't be roused
By any fear of danger once he's started
His own laying-out on this white sand.

Watching the usual landmarks in the sky,
He can no longer place them. Is that
Pegasus? Where's Orion? Surer of
The wash and whisper from the Maharees,
He spots the oyster-catcher going off
To raise the alarm: an insane Orpheus
Craving a past he'd never had. His quest
Beached here that started in mutilation
And manacled rubber-harvesters.

Suddenly it has thrown him on the ground,
A man sick with his past, middle-aged,
Mad, more or less, who waits to be lifted
High, kicking in mid-air, gurgling
For breath, swaying, while Banna's lonely sand
Drips for the last time from his shoe. So:
Was this the idea? The cure for every woe,
Injustice, brutishness? In this ecstasy
Larks rising everywhere, as he'd forgotten.

FRANK ORMSBY

The Builder

Even at fifty you were in demand,
three hayfields of your handiwork on show
each summer where your father's farm sloped
to the main road. So often we watched you step

into that rough circle. Your arms swept
round the prongs of dangerous pitchforks.
You seemed to embrace entire meadows,
patting them like aprons about your knees.

As you rose on your own foundation, people waved
from bus windows. The more you spread and trod,
above head-height, above hedge-height, the further we
had to step back not to lose sight of you.

You never looked like falling. Braced at the top,
you fielded the two hayropes, threw them back
nonchalantly between your legs
and prepared to return to the earth.

No memory now to match this: you gather your skirts
and slide with a girlish flourish
down the rick face,
land like a gymnast among our outstretched arms.

Snow

A white dot flicked back and forth across the bay window: not
A table-tennis ball, but 'ping-pong', since this is happening in another era,
The extended leaves of the dining-table – scratched mahogany veneer –
Suggesting many such encounters, or time passing: the celluloid diminuendo
As it bounces off into a corner and ticks to an incorrigible stop.
I pick it up days later, trying to get that pallor right: it's neither ivory
Nor milk. Chalk is better; and there's a hint of pearl, translucent
Lurking just behind opaque. I broke open the husk so many times
And always found it empty; the pith was a wordless bubble.

Though there's nothing in the thing itself, bits of it come back unbidden,
Playing in the archaic dusk till the white blip became invisible.
Just as, the other day, I felt the tacky pimples of a ping-pong bat
When the bank-clerk counted out my money with her rubber thimble, and knew
The black was bleeding into red. Her face was snow and roses just behind
The bullet-proof glass: I couldn't touch her if I tried. I crumpled up the chit –
No use in keeping what you haven't got – and took a stroll to Ross's auction.

There was this 'thirties scuffed leather sofa I wanted to make a bid for.
Gestures, prices: soundlessly collateral in the murmuring room.

I won't say what I paid for it: anything's too much when you have nothing.
But in the dark recesses underneath the cushions I found myself kneeling
As decades of the Rosary dragged by, the slack of years ago hauled up
Bead by bead; and with them, all the haberdashery of loss – cuff buttons,
Broken ball-point pens and fluff, old pennies, pins and needles, and yes,
A ping-pong ball. I cupped it in my hands like a crystal, seeing not
The future, but a shadowed parlour just before the blinds are drawn. Someone
Has put up two trestles. Handshakes all round, nods and whispers.
Roses are brought in, and suddenly, white confetti seethes against the window.

Jacta Est Alea

It was one of those puzzling necks of the wood where
the South was in the North, the way
The double cross in a jigsaw loops into its matrix,
like the border was a *clef*

With arbitrary teeth indented in it. Here, it cut clean
across the plastic
Lounge of The Half-Way House; my heart lay in
the Republic

While my head was in the Six, or so I was inclined.
You know that drinker's
Angle, elbow-propped, knuckles to his brow like one
of the Great Thinkers ?

He's staring at my throat in the Power's mirror,
debating whether
He should open up a lexicon with me: the price of
beer or steers, the weather.

We end up talking about talk. We stagger on the frontier.
He is pro. I am con.
Siamese-like, drunken, inextricable, we wade
into the Rubicon.

Of Difference Does It Make

During the 51-year existence of the Northern Ireland Parliament only one Bill sponsored by a non-Unionist member was ever passed.

Among the plovers and the stonechats
protected by the Wild Birds Act
of nineteen-hundred-and-thirty-one,
there is a rare stint called the notawhit
that has a schisty flight-call, like the chough's.
Notawhit, notawhit, notawhit
– it raps out a sharp code-sign
like a mild and patient prisoner
pecking through granite with a teaspoon.

Crannlaoch

(do Máirtín Ó Direáin)

Coigil do bhrí
A fhir an dáin
Coigil faoi thrí,
Bí i do chrann.

Sheas ar leac an tinteáin
Duilliúrdhánta ina láimh
Glór mar cheol toirní
Súil dharach an chrannlaoich.

Dearcán solais dár thuirling
De ruachraobh anuas
Phréamhaigh i ndán ar lár
Ár lomghoirtín is d'fhás.

Hearts of Oak

(for Máirtín Ó Direáin)

Save your breath,
Poem-maker.
Keep it under wraps
In the tall tree of yourself.

When he stood on the hearthstone
His hands would rustle with new poems.
A peal of thunder when he spoke.
His eye was a knot of oak.

A little acorn of light pitched
Into our bald patch
From the red branch above
Might take root there, and thrive.

translated by Paul Muldoon

Faith

My grandmother led us to believe in snow
as an old man in the sky shaking
feathers down from his mattress over the world.

Her bed in the morning was covered with tiny scales,
sloughed off in the night from peeling skin;
they floated in a cloud

of silver husks to the floor, or spun
in the open window like starry litter,
blowing along the road.

I burned them in a heap, a dream of coins
more than Thérèse's promised shower of roses,
or Virgil's souls, many as autumn leaves.

From the Dressing-Room

Left to itself, they say, every foetus
would turn female, staving in, nature
siding then with the enemy that
delicately mixes up genders. This
is an absence I have passionately sought,
brightening nevertheless my poet's attic
with my steady hands, calling him my blue
lizard till his moans might be heard
at the far end of the garden. For I like
his ways, he's light on his feet and does
not break anything, puts his entire soul
into bringing me a glass of water.

I can take anything now, even his being
away, for it always seems to me his
writing is for me, as I walk springless
from the dressing-room in a sisterly
length of flesh-coloured silk. Oh there
are moments when you think you can
give notice in a jolly, wifely tone,
tossing off a very last and sunsetty
letter of farewell, with strict injunctions
to be careful to procure his own lodgings:
that my good little room is lockable,
but shivery, I recover at the mere
sight of him propping up my pillow.

Ship of Death

(for my mother)

Watching you, for the first time,
turn to prepare your boat, my mother;
making it clear you have other business now –
the business of your future –
I was washed-through with anger.

It was a first survey,
an eye thrown
over sails, oars, timbers,
as many a time I'd seen that practised eye
scan a laden table.

How can you plan going off like this
when we stand at last, close enough, if the wind is right,
to hear what the other is saying?
I never thought you'd do this, turning away,
mid-sentence, your hand testing a rope,

your ear tuned
to the small thunder of the curling wave
on the edge of the great-night sea,
neither regretful nor afraid –
anxious only for the tide.

ROBERT JOHNSTONE

Notes for a Love Poem

Whatever it is, it ought to be
like an unpremeditated song,
obvious and value-free,

delineating all her shapes
to a Latin tune,
honouring her female hips

with the curves of a guitar,
woman tone,
a sunburst veneer,

and for her breasts
a gold saxophone
blown underneath the breath.

*

In terms of clothes
a gift of kirtles,
garlands, zones:

all I'd give would laud her in
a series of circles –
fresh cotton against her skin,

a blouse exposing her shoulders,
a gold ring, heavy bangles,
an anklet, a choker,

fetishes she'd decorously lose,
like nylons that crackle
and straps on her high-heel shoes.

The Cure for Warts

Had I been the seventh son of a seventh son
Living at the dead centre of a wood
Or at the dead end of a lane,
I might have cured by my touch alone
That pair of warts nippling your throat,

Who had no faith in a snail rubbed on your skin
And spiked on a thorn like a king's head,
In my spittle on shrunken stone,
In bathing yourself at the break of dawn
In dew or the black cock's or the bull's blood,

In other such secrets told by way of a sign
Of the existence of one or other god,
So I doubt if any woman's son
Could have cured by his touch alone
That pair of warts nibbling your throat.

Gathering Mushrooms

The rain comes flapping through the yard
like a tablecloth that she hand-embroidered.
My mother has left it on the line.
It is sodden with rain.
The mushroom shed is windowless, wide,
its high-stacked wooden trays
hosed down with formaldehyde.
And my father has opened the Gates of Troy
to that first load of horse manure.
Barley straw. Gypsum. Dried blood. Ammonia.
Wagon after wagon
blusters in, a self-renewing gold-black dragon

we push to the back of the mind.
We have taken our pitchforks to the wind.

All brought back to me that September evening
fifteen years on. The pair of us
tripping through Barnett's fair demesne
like girls in long dresses
after a hail-storm.
We might have been thinking of the fire-bomb
that sent Malone House sky-high
and its priceless collection of linen
sky-high.
We might have wept with Elizabeth McCrum.
We were thinking only of psilocybin.
You sang of the maid you met on the dewy grass –
And she stooped so low gave me to know
it was mushrooms she was gathering O.

He'll be wearing that same old donkey-jacket
and the sawn-off waders.
He carries a knife, two punnets, a bucket.
He reaches far into his own shadow.
We'll have taken him unawares
and stand behind him, slightly to one side.
He is one of those ancient warriors
before the rising tide.
He'll glance back from under his peaked cap
without breaking rhythm:
his coaxing a mushroom – a flat or a cup –
the nick against his right thumb;
the bucket then, the punnet to left or right,
and so on and so forth till kingdom come.

We followed the overgrown tow-path by the Lagan.
The sunset would deepen through cinnamon
to aubergine,
the wood-pigeon's concerto for oboe and strings,

allegro, blowing your mind.
And you were suddenly out of my ken, hurtling
towards the ever-receding ground,
into the maw
of a shimmering green-gold dragon.
You discovered yourself in some outbuilding
with your long-lost companion, me,
though my head had grown into the head of a horse
that shook its dirty-fair mane
and spoke this verse:

Come back to us. However cold and raw, your feet
were always meant
to negotiate terms with bare cement.
Beyond this concrete wall is a wall of concrete
and barbed wire. Your only hope
is to come back. If sing you must, let your song
tell of treading your own dung,
let straw and dung give a spring to your step.
If we never live to see the day we leap
into our true domain,
lie down with us now and wrap
yourself in the soiled grey blanket of Irish rain
that will, one day, bleach itself white.
Lie down with us and wait.

Aftermath

I

'Let us now drink,' I imagine patriot cry to patriot
after they've shot
a neighbor in his own aftermath, who hangs still between
two sheaves
like Christ between two tousle-headed thieves,
his body wired up to the moon, as like as not.

II

To the memory of another left to rot
near some remote beauty spot,
the skin of his right arm rolled up like a shirtsleeve,
let us now drink.

III

Only a few nights ago, it seems, they set fire to a big house
and it got
so preternaturally hot
we knew there would be no reprieve
till the swallows' nests under the eaves
had been baked into these exquisitely glazed little pots
from which, my love, let us now drink.

The Seamstress

I have a seamstress, making a shirt for me
In sultry weather, in the months we are together.

She measures my shoulders with tape, I feel on my back
The cool of her wooden yardstick, and submit

To a temporary contract, binding me
To the new and the strange. Together we lose ourselves

Among shades of blue, the melancholy feast
A culture of silkworms creates, as Chinese tailors

Stand and wait. For me it's the stuff of dreams,
For her a labour of love ... In her house on stilts

Where women are still slaves, she sews the collarless
Garment of pure freedom I have asked for

When I leave, keeping only for herself
Dry tailor's chalk, and the diagram of a body.

Child of the Empire

Last night I dreamt about Churchill.
He was smoking in the garden a big cigar.
Then the scene shifted and we both were
alone in a castle; a fire roared in the grate.

Portraits of lairds and merchant princes
looked down from the deep stairwell.
We talked about painting – his and others' –
and about failure;
how you've to live with that, too.

He coughed a good deal and his eyes clouded
as if he were going to tell me more
of Stalin perhaps, or the sick Roosevelt.
All I see now is the tartan slippers
with the little zipper down each side.

Ceist na Teangan

Cuirim mo dhóchas ar snámh
i mbáidín teangan
faoi mar a leagfá naíonán
i gcliabhán
a bheadh fite fuaite
de dhuilleoga feileastraim
is bitiúmin agus pic
bheith cuimilte lena thóin

ansan é a leagadh síos
i measc na ngiolcach
is coigeal na mban sí
le taobh na habhann,
féachaint n'fheadaraís
cá dtabharfaidh an sruth é,
féachaint, dála Mhaoise,
an bhfóirfidh iníon Fharoinn?

The Language Issue

I place my hope on the water
in this little boat
of the language, the way a body might put
an infant

in a basket of intertwined
iris leaves,
its underside proofed
with bitumen and pitch,

then set the whole thing down amidst
the sedge
and bulrushes by the edge
of a river

only to have it borne hither and thither,
not knowing where it might end up;
in the lap, perhaps,
of some Pharaoh's daughter.

translated by Paul Muldoon

Margadh na Gruaige

An raibh tú riamh ag margadh na gruaige?
Tá sé thíos ar dheis láimh le margadh na n-éan.
Caitheann tú triall go mall tré ghréasán de shráideanna cúnga
i mbaile beag Francach a bhaineann leis an Mheánaois.

Tá gleo is clampar ann is hurlamaboc.
Ceantálaithe ag glaoch amach os ard,
an praghas is airde á fhógairt acu go rábach,
iad ag díol is ag ceannach, ag cantáil ar gach slám.

Is chífidh tú trilseáin dualach' dualánach'
ag sníomh go talamh ann ina slaodaibh mín nó borb.
Cúilí réamhrá dho á n-ionramháil ie racaí;
giollaí á gcíoradh, banláimh i ndiaidh banláimhe.

An raibh tú riamh ag margadh na gruaige?
Do chuas-sa ann liom fhéin aon uair amháin.
Do gearradh díom m'fholt rua ó bhonn na cluaise
is díoladh ar phraghas ard é le sabhdán.

The Hair Market

Did you ever go to the Hair Market?
It's down on the right-hand side of the Bird Market.
You have to thread slowly through narrow streets
In a little medieval town in France.

It's there you'll hear the noise and fuss and uproar,
The auctioneers shouting over their megaphones,
Screaming the highest bid at the top of their voices,
Buying and selling, cutting deals at every turn.

And it's there you'll see plaits and chignons and ponytails
Flowing smooth or curling from ceiling to floor,
Heaps of tresses raked and teased out,
Servants combing them, armslength after armslength.

Were you ever in the Hair Market?
I went there once myself on a certain day.
They cut my long red locks close to my skull,
And sold them to a Sultan for the best price of all.

translated by Eiléan Ní Chuilleanáin

Wading

She's in the sea again.
She's got her white dress on.
She's wading through the waves
watched by no one.
The stars are blotted out
and the moon's hidden,
and she's splashing through the sea
thinking about him.

He was here an hour ago.
He ran along the beach.
He shouted out 'Julie!'
and waved a torch
but he never came her way
and she ignored him,
stood there and watched
as he staggered home.

Her eyes are pebbles.
Her dress is seaweed.
Her legs are driftwood
that needs to float,
but for now she keeps wading,
slicing the waves
that keep on offering
their myriad loves.

Silk

Should I tell you that just a century ago,
in the year of my father's – your granddad's – birth
the distribution of the silk industry
stretched as far as Tiverton to the west
and north to the looms and tenements of Paisley,

or that when, technically, silk is *thrown*
a single filament which is drawn unbroken
from the cocoon can measure a kilometre or more
and so, in this, it shares a subtle topology
with the network of veins beneath the skin,

which when stretched across, say, your collar-
or your pelvic-bone will reveal the bluish hues
of *Bombyx mori* eggs when they're freshly laid;
and since your skin has something too of the texture,
even the smell, of shantung and raw tussore

must I not then repeat to you the words of Count
Dandolo who, in his treatise on sericulture,
wrote of the worm itself: 'the greater the heat
in which it is hatched, the greater are its wants,
the more rapid its pleasures, the shorter its existence'?

Penance

And still they live in unforgiven places,
on the sides of arthritic hills,
where low walls hide the sea and the sea
hides the dead, though the dead still whisper
in their silent graves, 'I'm cold, I'm cold.'

Enough bog here to stoke the fires of Hell,
and stones so many you'd think they grew
in the soil. Though nothing ever grows.
God knows there was more wood on Calvary.

This morning, on a high road beyond Cleggan,
I passed the ruins of a deserted cottage,
and a ruined cottage that looked deserted,
only a man eyed me. I asked where the road went?
'To the end,' he said, 'the end.' Then shuffled off.

THOMAS MCCARTHY

The Wisdom of AE

Some days he would wander around his attic-room
in search of a recent letter or a new poem
that might have hitched from a rural Co-op,
or an unfinished painting that had desolately
hid between newspapers and a month of bills;
his life was full of things fresh or unmade

like the new country or a spring homestead.
He kept to his own chaos in the land of hot
views; opinion like a dagger couldn't disturb
his ways or alter his deepest occult reference.
(While the land was busy with war he was perturbed
by an incomplete vision of a future President.)

Visions came and went like shafts of sunlight
at the woods near Coole; nymphs playing on the shore
were part of a permanent familiar insight;
a familiar world of rocks, woods and water.
He was the first to live by the eternal Feminine,
to spill water and woodland over violent politics.

And his deepest vision was that feminine thought,
the lack of a killing view. His thoughts altered
the deepest enmities. Like a woman who gathers
her husband's arrogance into a basket of love,
he took our wars into the palm of his thought
and stroked the poisons from where we had fought.

Opals

Lying on my stomach,
silk pillows underneath me,
I trace the outline
of each plum blossom
on my sleeve
and try to hide my face
from the other ladies
with the screen of my hair.
They are discussing the Prince,
gossiping about which royal robe
suits him best.
I have traced the flower six times now,
hoping they won't ask me my opinion
or notice the handful of opal teardrops
decorating my sleeve.

DENNIS O'DRISCOLL

Water

The miracle of water
is that it tastes of nothing,
neither of chlorine nor peat,
nor of old tap fittings or dead sheep.

Water was the first mirror,
drinking images of beauty,
showing their wrinkled future
in the mildest breeze.

Water clings to its neutrality,
changes state at boiling point,
finds the level at which
tensions cool, limbs relax.

It is the splinter of ice in the heart,
the white blood of the snowman,
the burst main flooding
from Christ's frozen side.

The Flute Girl's Dialogue

Plato, come out now
with your sunburnt legs on ya
don't tell me to play to myself
or to the other women.

'Discourse in Praise of Love' indeed.

Bad mannered lot,
even if I cough when I come into the room
it does not stop your bleating.
That couch over there seats two comfortably
yet every time I enter
there's four of you on it
acting the maggot
then if Socrates walks in,
the way you all suck up to him.

Small wonder Plato
you have a leg to stand on
after all the red herrings
you put in people's mouths.
You hide behind Eryximachus
and suspend me like tired tattle.

'Tell the Flute Girl to go' indeed.

Let me tell you Big Sandals
the Flute Girl's had it.
When I get the sisters in here
we are going to sit on the lot of you,
come out then gushing platonic.

The Flute Girl knows
the fall of toga tune
the flick of tongue
salt-dip hemlock-sip
eye to the sky tune
hand on the thigh tune
moan and whimper talk
dual distemper talk.

When you played I listened,
when I play, prick up your ears.

PAULA MEEHAN

Child Burial

Your coffin looked unreal,
fancy as a wedding cake.

I chose your grave clothes with care,
your favourite stripey shirt,

your blue cotton trousers.
They smelt of woodsmoke, of October,

your own smell there too.
I chose a gansy of handspun wool,

warm and fleecy for you. It is
so cold down in the dark.

No light can reach you and teach you
the paths of wild birds,

the names of the flowers,
the fishes, the creatures.

Ignorant you must remain
of the sun and its work,

my lamb, my calf, my eaglet,
my cub, my kid, my nestling,

my suckling, my colt. I would spin
time back, take you again

within my womb, your amniotic lair,
and further spin you back

through nine waxing months
to the split seeding moment

you chose to be made flesh,
word within me.

I'd cancel the love feast
the hot night of your making.

I would travel alone
to a quiet mossy place,

you would spill from me into the earth
drop by bright red drop.

The Sea Urchin

She needs the spines
For dignity, her natural resistance
Along faintly bruised lines.
Deep inside the shell she is exposed
And glows or shivers
In her soft pink flesh.
This is also where she cries
With her hundred crescent eyes.

MOYA CANNON

Night

Coming back from Cloghane
in the sudden frost
of a November night,
I was ambushed
by the river of stars.

Disarmed by lit skies
I had utterly forgotten
this arc of darkness,
this black night
where the frost-hammered stars
were notes thrown from a chanter,
crans of light.

So I wasn't ready
for the dreadful glamour of Orion
as he struck out over Barr dTrí gCom
in his belt of stars.

At Gleann na nGealt
his bow of stars
was drawn against my heart.

What could I do?

Rather than drive into a pitch-black ditch
I got out twice,
leaned back against the car
and stared up at our windy, untidy loft
where old people had flung up old junk
they'd thought might come in handy,
ploughs, ladles, bears, lions, a clatter of heroes,
a few heroines, a path for the white cow, a swan
and, low down, almost within reach,
Venus, completely unfazed by the frost.

All Burials Are at Sea

Boats have been lifted down into the water all week now:
The centre-boards, the cabin cruisers, the great ocean-going,
And the toddlers are making heirlooms with their hands in the breakers.
Theirs is the drift of where he stands, my old shore-dwelling father
At his sea-front dormer window with the Second-World-War binoculars
Waiting for his life to well up like a submarine
So he can row out towards her, towards the dots and dashes,
Through the rowlocks' chronic bronchitis to the air of sirens,
And be among his countrymen at the bottom of the sea,
Feeling the pain of the oars like the start of a stroke in his shoulder
And sad for the living, for those left behind in the photographs.

He has stowed you in a little hardwood boat, a dug-out almost,
With a prayer-book full of your war kids shrieking Cheese
And a picture of Jesus dead to the world on a fishing-net, foetal,
While the wino mariners wail and the waves turn over the pages.
But the one that I cannot fathom floated in wetness before me,
A girl on a strand who is copying swimsuit stars in a movie,
The sweethearts of soldiers and sailors, a diver with jewellery on.

She has been buried two miles inland and two metres down
Where the tiny crustacean dust rises and rinses the
  wormholes.
For nothing omits it, that moment of coral, the violet,
  visible light
Or the jellyfish belling with joy through the dormitory
  suburbs.

Fíacha an tSolais

I mbathlach ceannslinne a chaith sé a shaol
leathbhealaigh i gcoinne Chnoc an tSéideáin;
druncaire, a raibh a dhreach is a dheilbh maol
agus lomchnámhach, macasamhail an screabáin
ina thimpeall, áit a bhfuarthas marbh é anuraidh
caite sa scrobarnach, lá polltach geimhridh:
a naoi mbliana fichead múchta ag ainíde dí,
is gan glór lena chaoineadh ach gocarsach cearc fraoigh.

Inniu, bhí fear an tsolais thuas ar bharr an tsímléara
ag scoitheadh sreanga leictreach. 'Tá'n bás,' ar seisean,
agus é ag meabhrú ar bhás anabaí an úinéara,
'amhail gearradh cumhachta. Ainneoin ár dtola a thig sé
de ghnáth. Ach an té a dhéanann faillí i bhfiacha an tsolais
nach follas go ndorchaíonn sé é féin d'aonturas.'

The E.S.B. Bill

In a slated cabin he spent his life,
half-way along the Hill of the Winds.
A drunk, his face and gait had the rough
and bare-boned character of scrub, of whins.
It was there he was found only last year,
emptied of life in the piercing winter;
his twenty-nine years drenched in beer –
his lament, a grouse's clucking despair.

Today the ESB man was at the chimney,
disconnecting the supply. 'Death,' he said,
(thinking of the young man so recently dead)
'death is like being cut off by the ESB –
the man who lets all his bills go unpaid
has already known the darkness of the dead.'

translated by Thomas McCarthy

Throwing the Beads

A mother at Shannon, waving to her young
Son setting out from North Kerry, flung
A rosary beads out to the tarmac
Suddenly as a lifebelt hurled from a pier.
Don't forget to say your prayers in Manhattan.
Dangling between ticket and visa,
She saw the bright crucifix among skyscrapers,
Shielding him from harm in streets out of serials,
Comforting as a fat Irish cop in a gangster film
Rattling his baton along a railing after dark.

For Jessica

The plastic basin hitched on your hip,
your arm falling outside, holding it
as you came down the garden,
was the tub you carried into the leasowes.

The wet damask had darkened,
but would dry to that bright fabric
you shook from the chest of drawers
and tautened, testing the winter.

As you go striding with that weight
across the water-meadows,
I glimpse your hem flailing seed-heads
and catching the goose-grass

you'll pluck out later at the fireside
where this new world takes hold.
The glow of a single spill
is carried in a cupped hand to the kindling

and we warm to the husbandry of words
such as russets from your childhood shire,
or a sportsfield known as the leasowes
where you raced through clover and vetchling.

MICHAEL O'LOUGHLIN

Latin as a Foreign Language

I suppose I should feel somehow vindicated
To see our declensions bite deeper
Than our legionaries' swords –
But somehow I don't.
We're a mixed lot here, devils
To drink; old senatorial types and
Discarded favourites, poets without patrons, etc.

When asked why they're here they might answer
About duty to the empire, missionary zeal
Or simply the spirit of adventure –
All rot, of course.
No one leaves Rome unless
He has to, or not exactly because he has to
Like a vulgar soldier in a press-ganged legion

But things somehow conspire to force him out.
Not all poets find patrons, not all
Fit smoothly into public life –
You know how it is.
One wrong word in the wrong ear,
One fateful opportunity fluffed, and
You may as well forget it. Who understands these things?

Some say they lie in the lap of the gods but either way
We end up here in the backwater of the empire
Drumming our illustrious tongue
Into barbarian skulls,
And polishing up the phrases
Of the oafs who govern in Rome's name.
Like I said, a mixed lot, refugees all from obscure failures.

Some marry local girls, and sprout blonde beards
And curls overnight. Poor bastards!

How can they take seriously
Those bovine bodies
And gaudy faces lisping bad breath.
Who could write poetry for such as these?
I think about these things a lot, but come to no conclusion.

During the freezing winter nights sitting round the wine
And olives, telling tales of sunnier days
Sucking ancient bits of gossip
Down to the dry pit
Cato elaborates his pet theory;
How Rome will someday crumble to dust
Beneath the barbarian heel, and only our precious language

Will survive, a frail silken line flung across the years.
But I don't know. Who among these barbarians
Would give a fart in his bearskin
For Horace or Virgil
Or any of us? All they want is enough
To haggle with a Sicilian merchant, or cheat
The Roman tax collector out of his rightful due.

But late at night, when I stumble out into
The sleet and cold I was not born to
And feel the threatening hug
Of those massive forests
Stuffed with nameless beasts
And the great godless northern sky
Threatening me with its emptiness and indifference

To me and all that are like me – then, sometimes
I think he may be right; that
We are the galley slaves
Sweating below
Bearing the beautiful
Princess who sits in the prow
Across the ocean to her unknown lover.

Modern Times

(for Seán Dunne)

I've a notion, instead of entering the hereafter
or turning into some mythical tree,
the spirits of dead shakers enter
the wood they fashioned with such severity.

The frigid, upright, spiny furniture
seems to withdraw as we intrude on each room
set so sparsely in this New Hampshire
ghost town that I can't imagine calling home.

And coming on their antique printer's shop,
with galley pages of *The Shaker Manifesto*
locked by the quoins so no character could drop,
I long for the security of such words.

But I've lost my quoin's key
and all my shaken words fall uneven.

The One Dim Thing

See, how he has turned to her, to that one spot
where her neck takes the light and whitens
to perfection: see how his finger strives to enter
that light and how, again, it is the same room, the same

heartbreaking light, the light of argument and desire,
the one illumination here: obsession's heaven,
the one dim thing relentlessly reached for,
the single gesture failing infinitely to accomplish itself.

He gives it up and settles back, he looks out the window
at the grey town: spires and rooftops, his own life creeping
like a burglar there. They lie absolutely still, the end of love
seeps through them like a drug, and because they are
  different

it works differently in each. She is drowsy now, almost
  asleep,
but his sceptical hands start out again, on their
ancient journey. They are not his hands now, they stray
  from him
like innocents, pilgrims who left the very hour

the faith shifted. Soon he will leave or she will,
and his hands will come back to him, days later, or weeks,
in the final scene. Much has yet to be decided:
whose room, what town, what exact degree of passion, pain.

In the end nothing of this may remain,
neither the room nor them, not a limb, not a single hair –
though the light I capture is the light they've left
and every shot is bereft . . .

A Pause

We are close now, it may be, to the delicate matter
which requires to be touched gently, if touched upon,
and for which all reserves of forethought and compassion
must lie ready to hand; neither to hurt nor flatter,
neither to let pass falsehoods nor to dissimulate,
and yet allow the substance to make itself apparent –
these are the special tactics of reserve and restraint
for which, and in which, patience is (so to speak) infinite.

The hesitation must arise from discomfort, even from pain,
a pause both taken and given; what will then emerge
may not in all decency be spoken of as yet,
although you may infer that its outline is sufficiently plain:
the imagination has enough here upon which to enlarge
in a quiet moment, and with such tact as it sees fit.

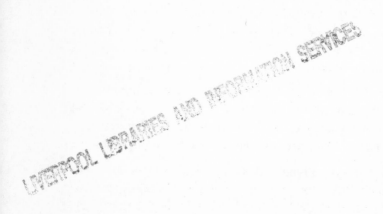

Acknowledgements

FERGUS ALLEN: 'Portrait of a Woman from the Fayum' from *Mrs Power Looks Over the Bay* (Faber & Faber, 1999), reprinted by permission of the publisher. SAMUEL BECKETT: 'Roundelay' from *Collected Poems* (John Calder, 1984). EAVAN BOLAND: 'The Black Lace Fan My Mother Gave Me' from *Collected Poems* (Carcanet, 1995), reprinted by permission of the publisher. JOSEPH CAMPBELL: 'Ad Limina' from *Poems of Joseph Campbell* (Allen Figgis & Co., 1963). CIARAN CARSON: 'Snow' from *The Ballad of HMS Belfast* (Gallery Press, 1999) and 'Jacta Est Alea' from *Opera et Cetera* (Gallery Press, 1996), reprinted by permission of the publisher. AUSTIN CLARKE: 'The Lost Heifer' and 'The Planter's Daughter' from *Collected Poems* (Dolmen Press/Oxford University Press, 1974), reprinted by permission of R. Dardis Clarke, 21 Pleasants Street, Dublin 8. HARRY CLIFTON: 'The Seamstress' from *Comparative Lives* (Gallery Press, 1982), reprinted by permission of the publisher. MICHAEL COADY: 'Letting Go' from *Oven Lane* (Gallery Press, 1987), reprinted by permission of the publisher. PADRAIC COLUM: 'She Moved Through the Fair' from *The Poet's Circuits: Collected Poems of Ireland* (Dolmen Press/Oxford University Press, 1960). TONY CURTIS: 'Penance' from *This Far North* (Dedalus Press, 1994). MICHAEL DAVITT: 'Crannlaoch'/'Hearts of Oak' (translated by Paul Muldoon) from *Selected Poems* (Raven Arts Press). GERALD DAWE: 'Child of the Empire' from *Heart of Hearts* (Gallery Press, 1995), reprinted by permission of the publisher. GREG DELANTY: 'Modern Times' from *The Hellbox* (Oxford University Press, 1999). SEAN DUNNE: 'Throwing the Beads' from *The Sheltered Nest* (Gallery Press, 1992), reprinted by permission of the publisher. PAUL DURCAN: 'In Memory: The Miami Showband: Massacred 31 July 1975', 'Birth of a Coachman' and 'The Hay Carrier' from *A Snail in My Prime* (Harvill Press, 1993). JOHN ENNIS: 'A Drink of Spring' from *A Drink of Spring* (Gallery Press, 1979), reprinted by permission of the publisher. PADRAIC FALLON: 'A Flask of Brandy' from *Collected Poems* (Carcanet Press, 1990), reprinted by permission of the publisher. PADRAIC FIACC: 'The British Connection' from *Ruined Pages: Selected Poems* (Blackstaff Press, 1994). LADY AUGUSTA GREGORY: 'Donal Og' from *Collected Works* (Colin Smythe). EAMON GRENNAN: 'Women Going' from *Selected & New Poems* (Gallery Press, 2000), reprinted by permission of the publisher. KERRY HARDIE: 'Ship of Death' from *A Furious Place* (Gallery Press, 1996), reprinted by permission of the publisher. MICHAEL HARTNETT: 'Death of an Irishwoman' from *A Farewell to English* (Gallery Press, 1975; enlarged 1978) and 'An Dobharchu Gonta'/'The Wounded Otter' from *A Necklace of Wrens* (Gallery Press, 1987), reprinted by permission of the publisher. SEAMUS HEANEY: 'Mossbawn: Two Poems in Dedication: Sunlight', 'Casualty' and 'The Harvest Bow' from *New Selected Poems 1966–1987* (Faber & Faber, 1990), reprinted by permission of the publisher. JOHN

HEWITT: 'Substance and Shadow' and 'A Local Poet' from *The Collected Poems of John Hewitt* (The Blackstaff Press, 1991). RITA ANN HIGGINS: 'The Flute Girl's Dialogue' from *Higher Purchase* (Salmon Publishing, 1996). PEARSE HUTCHINSON: 'Into Their True Gentleness' from *Selected Poems* (Gallery Press, 1982), reprinted by permission of the publisher. VALENTIN IREMONGER: 'The Toy Horse' from *New & Selected Poems* (Dedalus Press). ROBERT JOHNSTONE: 'Notes for a Love Poem' from *Breakfast in a Bright Room* (The Blackstaff Press). JAMES JOYCE: 'Tilly' from *Pomes Penyeach* (1927), copyright the Estate of James Joyce, reproduced with the permission of the Estate of James Joyce from *James Joyce: Poems and Shorter Writings*. PATRICK KAVANAGH: 'Innocence', 'Epic' and 'In Memory of my Mother' from *Selected Poems* (Penguin Books, 2000). BRENDAN KENNELLY: 'Bread' from *A Time for Voices: Selected Poems 1960–1990* (Bloodaxe Books, 1990). THOMAS KINSELLA: 'Hen Woman' and 'Wyncote, Pennsylvania: A Gloss' from *Collected Poems, 1956–2001* (Carcanet Press, 2001), reprinted by permission of the publisher. SEAN LYSAGHT: 'For Jessica' from *Scarecrow* (Gallery Press, 1998), reprinted by permission of the publisher. THOMAS MCCARTHY: 'The Wisdom of AE' from *The Sorrow Garden* (Anvil Press Poetry). DONAGH MACDONAGH: 'Just an Old Sweet Song' from *A Warning to Conquerors* (Dolmen Press, 1968). PATRICK MACDONOGH: 'Over the Water' from *Our Landscape Still* (Secker & Warburg, 1958), reprinted by permission of Gallery Press on behalf of the Estate of Patrick MacDonogh. PETER MCDONALD: 'A Pause' from *Adam's Dream* (Bloodaxe Books). MEDBH MCGUCKIAN: 'Faith' and 'From the Dressing-Room' from *Selected Poems* (Gallery Press, 1997), reprinted by permission of the publisher. TOM MACINTYRE: 'Kisses' from *A Glance Will Tell You and A Dream Confirm* (Dedalus Press). LOUIS MACNEICE: 'Mayfly', 'Brother Fire' and 'Charon' from *Collected Poems* (Faber & Faber, 1979). DEREK MAHON: 'The Studio', 'A Disused Shed in Co. Wexford' and 'Tractatus' from *Collected Poems* (Gallery Press, 1999), reprinted by permission of the publisher. AIDAN MATHEWS: 'All Burials are at Sea' from *According to the Small Hours* (Jonathan Cape, 1998), reprinted by permission of The Random House Group Ltd. PAULA MEEHAN: 'Child Burial' from *The Man Who Was Marked By Winter* (Gallery Press, 1991), reprinted by permission of the publisher. MAIRE MHAC AN TSAOI: 'Athdheirdre'/'A Second Deirdre' (translated by Patrick Crotty) from *Margadh na Saoire* (Sairseal agus Dill). JOHN MONTAGUE: 'All Legendary Obstacles' and 'A Bright Day' from *Collected Poems* (Gallery Press, 1995), reprinted by permission of the publisher. PAUL MULDOON: 'The Cure for Warts', 'Gathering Mushrooms' and 'Aftermath' from *Poems 1968–1998* (Faber & Faber, 2001), reprinted by permission of the publisher. RICHARD MURPHY: 'Stormpetrel' and 'Sunup' from *Collected Poems* (Gallery Press, 2000), reprinted by permission of the publisher. EILEAN NI CHUILLEANAIN: 'Fireman's Lift' and 'Studying the Language' from *The*

Brazen Serpent (Gallery Press, 1994), reprinted by permission of the publisher. NUALA NI DHOMHNAILL: 'Ceast na Teangan'/'The Language Issue' (translated by Paul Muldoon) from *The Pharaoh's Daughter* (Gallery Press, 1990) and 'Margadh na Graige'/'The Hair Market' (translated by Eilean ni Chuilleanain) from *The Water Horse* (Gallery Press, 1999), reprinted by permission of the publisher. JULIE O'CALLAGHAN: 'Opals' from *Edible Anecdotes & Other Poems* (Dolmen Press, 1983). FRANK O'CONNOR: 'Advice to Lovers' from *The Little Monasteries* (Colin Smythe, 1976). MAIRTIN O DIREAIN: 'Glor Acastora'/'Axle Song' (translated by Tomas Mac Siomoin and Douglas Sealy) from *Selected Poems* (The Goldsmith Press). BERNARD O'DONOGHUE: 'Casement on Banna' from *The Weakness* (Chatto & Windus, 1991), reprinted by permission of The Random House Group Ltd. DENNIS O'DRISCOLL: 'Water' from *Quality Time* (Anvil Press Poetry, 1997), reprinted by permission of the author. MICHAEL O'LOUGHLIN: 'Latin as a Foreign Language' from *The Diary of a Silence* (Raven Arts Press). MARY O'MALLEY: 'The Sea Urchin' from *The Knife in the Wave* (Salmon Publishing, 1997). SEAN O RIORDAIN: 'Malairt'/'Mirror' (translated by Ciaran Carson) and 'Reo'/'Frost' (translated by Maurice Riordan) from *Brosna* (Sairseal agus Dill). FRANK ORMSBY: 'The Builder', published in *The Irish Review*. CATHAL O SEARCAIGH: 'Fiacha an tSolais'/'The E.S.B. Bill' (translated by Thomas McCarthy) from *Selected Poems* (Clo Iar-Chonnachta Teo). TOM PAULIN: 'Of Difference Does It Make' from *Liberty Tree* (Faber & Faber, 1983), reprinted by permission of the publisher. MAURICE RIORDAN: 'Silk' from *Floods* (Faber & Faber, 2000), reprinted by permission of the publisher. W. R. RODGERS: 'Field Day' from *Poems* (Gallery Books, 1993), reprinted by permission of the publisher. JAMES SIMMONS: 'From the Irish' from *Poems 1956–1986* (Gallery Press, 1986), reprinted by permission of the publisher. PETER SIRR: 'The One Dim Thing' from *Ways of Falling* (Gallery Press, 1991), reprinted by permission of the publisher. JAMES STEPHENS: 'The Goat Paths' from *Collected Poems* (Macmillan, 1926; revised, 1954), reprinted by permission of The Society of Authors as the Literary Representative of the Estate of James Stephens. MATTHEW SWEENEY: 'Wading' from *A Smell of Fish* (Jonathan Cape). HELEN WADDELL: 'For France' from *More Latin Lyrics* (Victor Gollancz). W. B.YEATS: 'The Wild Swans at Coole', 'Broken Dreams' 'To a Squirrel at Kyle-na-no', 'Easter 1916', 'A Last Confession' and 'High Talk' from *Collected Poems* (Picador, 1990), reprinted by permission of A. P. Watt Ltd on behalf of Michael B. Yeats.

Every effort has been made to trace or contact all copyright holders. The publishers would be pleased to rectify any omissions brought to their notice at the earliest opportunity.

Index of Poets